Presented to

_____

FROM:

_____

DATE:

Celebrate Christmas
And the Beautiful Traditions of Advent

WHITE STONE BOOKS
LAKELAND, FLORIDA

Celebrate Christmas
And the Beautiful Traditions of Advent
ISBN 1-59379-028-7
Copyright © Bob and Kelli James
BrainChild Creative Services
Winchester, Oklahoma

Published by White Stone Books, Inc.
P.O. Box 2835
Lakeland, Florida 33806

09 08 07 06 05   10 9 8 7 6 5 4 3 2 1

Celebrate Christmas

And the Beautiful
Traditions of Advent

Contents

Introduction

Advent means "coming" or "arrival." During the Advent season we joyously and prayerfully anticipate the celebration of Jesus' first advent. And we look forward to His second advent, while we affirm that He is indeed present in the world today offering His redeeming love to anyone who will simply receive it.

> *"For a child is born to us, a son is given to us. And the government will rest on his shoulders. These will be his royal titles: Wonderful Counselor, Mighty God, Everlasting Father, Prince of Peace. His ever expanding, peaceful government will never end. He will rule forever with fairness and justice from the throne of his ancestor David. The passionate commitment of the Lord Almighty will guarantee this!"*
>
> ISAIAH 9:6-7 NLT

Over the course of the next twenty-five days, this book will show you how each of the traditions and symbols of the season ultimately point to our redemption through our Savior—Jesus Christ—and His Father—our Father—who sent His only Son to live and die for us. It will change the way you view Christmas, thus enabling you to focus on the true and powerful meaning of the season and cause your heart to rejoice in the fact that God has redeemed mankind—and that is the beautiful story of Christmas.

The traditional, liturgical season of Advent varies in date and number of days each year. It begins on the fourth Sunday before Christmas day and ends on Christmas Eve.

We have chosen a simplified observance, similar to a traditional Advent calendar, using the dates of December 1st through December 25th.

Each day you'll have the opportunity to participate in a step toward advent with your family, and a prayer for the day. Lastly, each advent step and prayer is followed with a touching story or scripture reading that you can read with your family and further fix your focus on the true joys of the Advent season.

This Christmas, open your heart anew to the celebration of the holiday and may your Christmas season be full of rejoicing in our Great Redeemer!

Celebrate Christmas

And the Beautiful
Traditions of Advent

December 1

The Advent Calendar

AS YOU EMBARK upon this most joyous season, bring a spirit of hope and expectation to the celebration of Advent by hanging an Advent calendar where your family often gathers, such as the kitchen or dining room.

You can purchase your own Advent calendar online or at any local bookstore during the Christmas season. Pre-made Advent calendars are available in many styles and sizes. If you have the time and feel inspired, you can make your own. Some Advent calendars display symbols from the Old Testament on each day, so you can talk to your family about the significance of each day's symbol. For small children, try personalizing your calendar by affixing a favorite piece of candy to each day. Be creative and make it fun!

Heavenly Father,

As we begin this Advent season, let us be ever mindful of Your love for us. Your great love is why You sent Your Son to live and die on this earth, in our world. He became a man, flesh and blood, like us so that He could experience life through our eyes—the joys and triumphs as well as the temptations and pains.

May this Advent season serve as a daily reminder that Jesus came, but also that He died and rose again, that He is still with us everywhere we go and in everything we do. Show us how to share the love You have given us with others. We ask for opportunities today, as a family and individually, to express Your love to whoever You bring across our path— a friend, a family member, or a complete stranger.

And we pray tonight for our family and friends, and whoever you may bring to our remembrance: "The Lord bless you and keep you; the Lord make his face shine upon you and be gracious to you; the Lord turn his face toward you and give you peace" (NUMBERS 6:24-26.).

Thank You so much, Father God, for this precious gift. May our gratitude rise up in joyous worship to Your throne.

In Jesus' precious name,

Amen

Christmas Day in the Morning

By Pearl S. Buck

HE WOKE SUDDENLY and completely. It was four o'clock, the hour at which his father had always called him to get up and help with the milking. Strange how the habits of his youth clung to him still! That was fifty years ago, and his father had been dead for thirty, yet he waked at four o'clock every morning. Over the years, he had trained himself to turn over and go to sleep, but this morning it was Christmas.

Why did he feel so awake tonight? He slipped back in time, as he did so easily nowadays. He was fifteen years old and still on his father's farm. He loved his father. He had not known it until one day a few days before Christmas, when he had overheard his father talking to his mother.

"Mary, I hate to wake Rob in the mornings. He's growing so fast and he needs his sleep. If you could see how hard he's sleeping when I go in to wake him up! I wish I could manage alone."

"Well, you can't Adam." His mother's voice was brisk, "Besides, he isn't a child anymore. It's time he took his turn."

"Yes," his father said slowly. "But I sure do hate to wake him."

When he heard his father's words, something in him spoke: His father loved him! He had never thought of that before, simply taking for granted the tie of their blood. Neither his father nor his mother talked about loving their children—they had no time for such things. There was always so much to do on the farm.

Now that he knew his father loved him, there would be no loitering in the mornings and having to be called again. He always got up immediately after that. He stumbled blindly in his sleep and pulled on his clothes with his eyes shut, but he got up.

And then on the night before Christmas, that year when he was fifteen, he lay for a few minutes thinking about the next day. They were poor, and most of the excitement about Christmas was in the turkey they had raised themselves and the mince pies his mother had made. His sisters sewed presents for everyone and his mother and father always bought him something he needed, like a warm jacket, but usually something more too, such as a book. And he saved and bought them each something, too.

He wished, that Christmas when he was fifteen, he had a better present for his father. As usual he had gone to the ten-cent store and bought a tie. It had seemed nice enough until he lay thinking the night before Christmas. As he gazed out of his attic window, the stars were bright.

"Dad," he had once asked when he was a little boy, "What is a stable?"

"It's just a barn," his father had replied, "like ours."

Then Jesus had been born in a barn, and to a barn the shepherds had come.

The thought struck him like a silver dagger. Why couldn't he give his father a special gift too, out there in the barn? He could get up early, earlier than four o'clock, and he could creep into the barn and do all the milking before his father even got out of bed. He'd do it all alone, milk the cows and clean up, and then when his father went in to start the milking he'd see it all was done. And he would know who had done it. He laughed to himself as he looked at the stars. It was what he would do! He musn't sleep too sound and forget to get up early.

He must have waked twenty times, scratching a match each time to look at his old watch—midnight, half past one, then two o'clock.

At a quarter to three he got up and put on his clothes. He crept downstairs, careful to avoid the creaky boards, and let himself out. The cows looked at him, sleepy and surprised. It was early for them too.

He had never milked all alone before, but it seemed almost easy. He kept thinking about his father's surprise. His father would come in to get him, saying that he would get things started while Rob was getting dressed. He'd go to the barn, open the door, and then he'd go get the two big empty milk cans waiting to be filled. But they wouldn't be waiting or empty, they'd be standing in the milk house, filled.

"What on earth!" he could hear his father exclaiming.

He smiled and milked steadily, two strong streams rushing into the pail, frothing and fragrant.

The task went more easily than he had ever known it to go before. For once, milking was not a chore. It was something else, a gift to his father who loved him. He finished, the two milk cans were full, and he covered them and closed the milk house door carefully, making sure to close the latch.

Back in his room he had only a minute to pull off his clothes in the darkness and jump into bed, for he heard his father up and moving around. He put the covers over his head to silence his quick breathing. The door opened.

"Rob," his father called. "We have to get up, son, even if it is Christmas."

"Aw-right," he said sleepily.

His father closed the door and he lay still, laughing to himself. In just a few minutes his father would know. His dancing heart was ready to jump from his body.

The minutes were endless—ten, fifteen, he did not know how many, it seemed like hours—and he heard his father's footsteps again. When his father opened the door he lay perfectly still.

"Rob!"

"Yes, Dad?"

His father was laughing, a strange sobbing sort of laugh.

"Thought you'd fool me, did you?" His father was standing by his bed, feeling for him, pulling away the covers.

"Merry Christmas, Dad!"

He found his father and clutched him in a great hug. He felt his father's arms wrap around him. It was dark and they could not see each other's faces.

"Son, I thank you. Nobody ever did a nicer thing...."

"Oh, Dad, I want you to know—I do want to be good!" The words broke from him of their own will. He did not know what to say. His heart was bursting with love.

He got up and pulled on his clothes again and they went down to the Christmas tree. Oh, what a Christmas, and how his heart had nearly burst again with shyness and pride as his father told his mother and sisters about how he, Rob, had got up all by himself and finished all the milking.

"The best Christmas gift I ever had, and I'll remember it, son, every year on Christmas morning, so long as I live."

They had both remembered it every year, and now that his father was dead, he remembered it alone: that blessed Christmas dawn when, alone with the cows in the barn, he had made his first gift of true love.

This Christmas he wanted to write a card to his wife and tell her how much he loved her. It had been a long time since he had really told her, although he loved her in a very special way, much more than he ever had when they were young. He had been fortunate that she had loved him. Ah, that was the true joy of life, the ability to love. Love was still alive in him, it still was.

It occurred to him suddenly that it was alive because long ago it had been born in him when he knew his father loved him. That was it: Love alone could awaken love. And he could give the gift again and again. This morning, this blessed Christmas morning, he would give it to his beloved wife. He would write it down in a letter for her to read and keep forever. He went to his desk and began to write: My dearest love....

Such a happy, happy, Christmas!

December 2

Placing of the Advent Wreath

ONE OF THE MOST beautiful and evocative symbols of the Advent season is the traditional Advent wreath. You can create your own unique Advent wreath along with your family by adding candles, bows, and other creative adornments to a real or artificial evergreen wreath.

The circular evergreen wreath symbolizes God's never ending love and grace. The candles—typically three purple and one rose—represent hope, peace, joy, and love. Real wreaths made from yew, pine, cedar, fir, laurel, and holly are especially fragrant and lovely. Once you have decorated your wreath, set aside a special time as a family to display it in a place of honor on your table, hearth, or mantle.

Father God,

As we commemorate this Advent season with a symbol of Your everlasting love help us to remember Your promises. We thank You for Your grace toward us, that while we were still sinners, Jesus died for us. (See Romans 5:8.) May the evergreen's nature remind us of the everlasting life we've been given in You. Our leaf will not wither or fade because we are planted by rivers of water and everything we do will prosper. (See Psalm 1:3.)

May we be ever mindful of all the gifts You've given us—the hope of eternal life, the peace of mind and heart, the joy that gives us strength, and the love that makes us whole. Thank You for making us Your children. Thank You for the contentment and peace that come from resting in Your care.

When the stress of the Christmas season tries to overwhelm us, we will cast the whole of our care on You, because we know that You care for us. (See 1 Peter 5:7.)

In Jesus' wonderful name,

Amen ✾

The Lost Word
Part One

Adapted from "The Lost Word" by Henry Van Dyke

"COME DOWN, HERMAS, come down! The night is past. It is time to be stirring. Christ is born today. Peace be with you in His name. Make haste and come down!"

A little group of young men were standing in a street of Antioch, in the dusk of early morning, fifteen hundred years ago—a class of candidates who had nearly finished their years of training for the Christian church. They had come to call their fellow student Hermas from his lodging.

But Hermas was not asleep. He had been waking for hours, and the walls of his narrow lodging had been a prison to his heart. A nameless sorrow and discontent had fallen upon him, and he could find no escape from the heaviness of his own thoughts.

Hermas was out of tune with everything around him. He had been thinking, through the dead night, of all that he had given up when he left the house of his father, the wealthy pagan Demetrius, to join the company of the Christians. Only two years ago he had been one of the richest young men in Antioch. Now he was one of the poorest. The worst of it was that, though he had made the choice willingly and with a kind of enthusiasm, he was already dissatisfied with it. Doubtless he had found the true religion, but he had found it only as a task and a burden; its joy and peace had slipped away from him.

"Come down, Hermas, you sluggard! Come down! It is Christmas morn. Awake, and be glad with us!"

"I am coming," he answered listlessly; "only have patience a moment. I have been awake since midnight, and waiting for the day."

"You hear him!" said his friends one to another. "How he puts us all to shame! He is more watchful, more eager, than any of us. Our master, John the Presbyter, does well to be proud of him. He is the best man in our class."

The great city, still chiefly pagan, lay more than half asleep. But multitudes of the Christians, dressed in white and carrying lighted torches in their hands, were hurrying toward the Basilica of Constantine to keep the new holy day of the church, the festival of the birthday of their Master.

The church was soon crowded, and the younger converts found it difficult to come to their appointed place. A touch here, a courteous nod there, a little patience, a little persistence, and at last they stood in their place. Hermas was taller than his companions; he could look easily over their heads and survey the sea of people stretching away through the columns.

The call to prayer sounded down the long aisle. Thousands of hands were joyously lifted in the air, and the "Amen" was like the murmur of countless ripples in an echoing place. Then the singing began, led by the choir of a hundred trained voices which the Bishop Paul had founded in Antioch. Hermas had often been carried on those

Tides of music's golden sea
Sailing toward eternity.

But today his heart was a rock that stood motionless. The flood passed by and left him unmoved.

Then the teacher, John of Antioch, rose to speak. He played on that immense congregation as a master on an instrument. He rebuked their sins, and they trembled. He touched their sorrows, and they wept. He spoke of the conflicts, the triumphs, the glories of their faith, and they broke out in thunders of applause. He hushed them into reverent silence, and led them tenderly, with the wise men of the East, to the lowly birthplace of Jesus.

But the soul of Hermas did not answer. He was out of sympathy with the eager preacher, the joyous hearers. In their harmony he had no part. Was it for this that he had forsaken his inheritance and narrowed his life to poverty and hardship? What was it all worth?

The gracious prayers with which the young converts were blessed and dismissed before the sacrament sounded hollow in his ears. Never had he felt so utterly lonely as in that praying throng. He went out with his companions like a man departing from a banquet where all but he had been fed.

"Farewell, Hermas," they cried, as he turned from them at the door. But he did not look back, nor wave his hand. He was already alone in his heart.

He went out of the city by the Western Gate, under the golden cherubim that the Emperor Titus had stolen from the ruined Temple of Jerusalem and fixed upon the arch of triumph. He turned to the left, and climbed the hill to the road that led to the Grove of Daphne.

Hermas found the grove quite deserted. There was no sound in the enchanted vale but the rustling of the wind through the laurel thickets, and the babble of innumerable streams. He sat down beside a gushing spring, and gave himself up to sadness.

How beautiful the world would be, Hermas thought, *how joyful, how easy to live in, without religion! These questions about unseen things, these restraints and duties and sacrifices—if I were only free from them all, and could only forget them all, then I could live my life as I pleased, and be happy.*

"Why not?" said a quiet voice at his back.

He turned, and saw an old man with a long beard and a threadbare cloak standing behind him and smiling curiously.

"How is it that you answer that which has not been spoken?" said Hermas. "And who are you that honor me with your company?"

"Forgive the intrusion," answered the stranger; "it is not ill meant. A friendly interest is as good as an introduction."

"But to what singular circumstance do I owe this interest?"

"To your face," said the old man. "Perhaps also a little to the fact that I am the oldest inhabitant here, and feel as if all visitors were my guests, in a way."

"Are you, then, one of the keepers of the grove?"

"My profession is the care of altars. In fact, I am the solitary priest of Apollo whom the Emperor Julian found here when he came to revive the worship of the grove, some twenty years ago. How many altars do you think there have been in this grove?"

"I do not know."

"Just four-and-twenty. I have had something to do with most of them in my time. They are transitory. They give employment to caretakers for a while. But the thing that lasts, and the thing that interests me, is the human life that plays around them. Life is a game, and the world keeps it up merrily. But you? You are of a sad countenance for one so young and so fair. Are you a loser in the game?"

The words and tone of the speaker fitted Hermas' mood as a key fits the lock. He opened his heart to the old man, and told him the story of his life: his luxurious boyhood in his father's house; the irresistible spell which compelled him to forsake it when he heard John's preaching of the new religion; his lonely year with the anchorites among the mountains; the strict discipline in his teacher's house at Antioch; his weariness of duty, his distaste for poverty, his discontent with worship.

"And today," said he, "I have been thinking that I am a fool. My life is swept as bare as a hermit's cell. There is nothing in it but a dream, a thought of God, which does not satisfy me."

"Well," said the old man, soothingly, as he plucked a leaf from the laurel tree above them and dipped it in the spring, "let us dismiss the riddles of belief. You know this is a Castalian fountain. The Emperor Hadrian once read his fortune here from a leaf dipped in the water. Let us see what this leaf tells us. It is already turning yellow. How do you read that?"

"Wealth," said Hermas, laughing.

"And here is a tracing of wreaths upon the surface. What do you make of that?"

"What you will," said Hermas, not even taking the trouble to look. "Suppose we say success and fame?"

"Yes," said the stranger; "it is all written here. I promise that you shall enjoy it all. There is only one thing that I ask. This is the season that you Christians call Christmas and you have taken up the custom of exchanging gifts. Well, if I give to you, you must give to me. It is a small thing, and really the thing you can best afford to part with: a single word—the name of Him you profess to worship. Let me take that word and all that belongs to it entirely out of your life, so that you shall never hear it or speak it again. I promise you everything, and this is all I ask in return. Do you consent?"

"Yes. I consent," said Hermas, mocking. "If you can take your price, a word, you can keep your promise, a dream."

The stranger laid the long, cool, wet leaf softly across the young man's eyes. An icicle of pain darted through them; every nerve in his body was drawn together there in a knot of agony. Then all the tangle of pain seemed to be lifted out of him and he sank into a profound sleep.

The break with the old life was as clean as if it had been cut with a knife. Some faint image of a hermit's cell, a bare lodging in a back street of Antioch, a classroom full of earnest students, remained in Hermas' memory. Some dull echo of the voice of John the Presbyter still lingered in his ears; but it was like something that had happened to another person, something that he had read long ago, but of which he had lost the meaning.

Hermas' father had died and he was called upon to take over his estate. His new life was full and smooth and rich—too rich for any sense of loss to make itself felt. Nothing needed to be considered, prepared for, begun. Everything was ready and waiting for him. All that he had to do was to go on.

The period of mourning for his father came at a fortunate moment to seclude and safeguard him from the storm of political troubles and persecutions that fell upon Antioch in the year 387. The friends of his father, prudent and conservative persons, gathered around Hermas and made him welcome to their circle. Chief among them was Libanius, his nearest neighbor, whose daughter Athenais had been Hermas' playmate in the old days.

He had left her a child. He found her a beautiful woman. "Where have you been, these two years?" said Athenais, as they walked together through the garden of lilies where they had so often played.

"In a land of tiresome dreams," answered Hermas; "but you have wakened me, and I am never going back again." The love of Athenais and Hermas was like a tiny rivulet that sinks out of sight in a cavern, but emerges again a bright and brimming stream. The careless comradery of childhood was mysteriously changed into a complete companionship.

When Athenais entered the House of the Golden Pillars as a bride, all the music of life came with her. Day after day, night after night, week after week, month after month, the bliss of the home unfolded like a rose of a thousand leaves. When a child came to them, a strong, beautiful boy, the heart of the rose was filled with overflowing fragrance. Happiness was heaped upon happiness.

Strangely enough, all of his good fortune began to press upon Hermas, to trouble him with the very excess of joy. He felt as if there were something yet needed to complete and secure it all. There was an urgency within him to find some expression and culmination of his happiness.

He spoke of it to Athenais, as they sat together, one summer evening, with their boy playing at their feet. "I, too, have felt it, Hermas, this burden, this need, this unsatisfied longing. I think I know what it means. It is gratitude. There is no perfect joy without gratitude. But we have never learned it, and the want of it troubles us. We must find the word for it, and say it together. Then we shall be perfectly joined in perfect joy. Come, my dear lord, let us take the boy with us, and give thanks."

Hermas lifted the child in his arms, and turned with Athenais into the depth of the garden. The tones of Hermas were clear and low as he began, half-speaking and half-chanting, in the rhythm of an ancient song:

"Wide is our world; we are rich; we have all things. Life is abundant within us—a measureless deep. Deepest of all is our love, and it longs to speak.

"Come, thou final word; Come, thou crown of speech! Come, thou charm of peace! Open the gates of our hearts. Lift the weight of our joy and bear it upward.

"For all good gifts, for all perfect gifts, for love, for life, for the world, we praise, we bless, we thank—"

As a soaring bird, struck by an arrow, falls headlong from the sky, so the song of Hermas fell. At the end of his flight of gratitude there was nothing—a blank, a hollow space.

"Let us go back," he said sadly to Athenais; "the child is heavy upon my shoulder. We will lay him to sleep, and go into the library. The air grows chilly. We were mistaken. The gratitude of life is only a dream. There is no one to thank."

And in the garden it was already night.

December 3

Lighting of the First Candle in the Advent Wreath

THE FIRST CANDLE of the Advent wreath symbolizes hope or expectation. It represents both the eager anticipation of a coming Messiah woven throughout the Old Testament and the promise that Jesus would return to earth to claim His faithful ones threaded throughout the New Testament.

Take a moment to contemplate the wonder of Christ's birth and the hope of His soon return as you gather your family to light the first candle of the Advent wreath. Family dinner is a particularly poignant time to observe the lighting of the Advent candles. Invite your family members to share a scripture or recount a portion of the Christmas story surrounding the theme of hope as you share this special tradition together.

Dear Lord,

We come to You today in gratitude. We are grateful that we know Your name and the name of Your Son, for there is no other name under heaven that can save us. (SEE ACTS 4:12.). *We thank You for the hope we have found in You. We pray that we can share that hope with others, the hope of Your salvation, the hope of Your coming again, the hope of peace and joy in Your presence.*

Lord, remind us to pass on our hope to the next generation by telling them of Your wonderful works, so that they will put their trust in You and not forget Your deeds but keep Your commands. (SEE PSALM 78:7.)

God, You are so good to us. We pray that we would remember that throughout this season. Let Your goodness to us flow through us and touch everyone we meet.

We love You, Lord.

Amen

The Lost Word
Part Two

Adapted from "The Lost Word" by Henry Van Dyke

THE NEXT MORNING the old man whom he had seen in the Grove of Daphne, but never since, appeared mysteriously at the door of the house, as if he had been sent for, and entered like an invited guest.

Hermas could not but make him welcome, and at first he tried to regard him with reverence and affection as the one through whom fortune had come. But it was impossible. There was a chill in the smile of Marcion, as he called himself, that seemed to mock at reverence. In his presence Hermas was conscious of a certain irritation, a resentful anger against the calm, cold scrutiny of the eyes that followed him everywhere.

"Why do you look at me so curiously?" asked Hermas, one morning, as they sat together in the library. "Do you see anything strange in me?"

"No," answered Marcion, "something familiar."

"And what is that?"

"A singular likeness to a discontented young man that I met some years ago in the Grove of Daphne."

"But why should that interest you? Surely it was to be expected."

"A thing that we expect often surprises us when we see it. Besides, my curiosity is piqued. I suspect you of keeping a secret from me."

"You are jesting with me. There is nothing in my life that you do not know. What is the secret?"

"Nothing more than the wish to have one. You are growing tired of your bargain. The play wearies you. That is foolish. Do you want to try a new part?"

"You are right," said Hermas. "I am tired. We have been going on stupidly in this house, as if nothing was possible but what my father had done before me."

"You are speaking again like a man after my own heart," said the old man. There is no folly but the loss of an opportunity to enjoy a new sensation."

From that day Hermas seemed to be possessed with a perpetual haste, an uneasiness that left him no repose. The world might have nothing better to give than it had already given; but surely it had many things that were new, and Marcion should help him to find them.

Under his learned counsel, the House of the Golden Pillars took on a new magnificence. Artists were brought from Corinth and Rome and Alexandria to adorn it with splendor. Its fame glittered around the world. Banquets of incredible luxury drew the most celebrated guests into its dining hall, and filled them with envious admiration. Everything that Hermas touched prospered. He bought a tract of land in the Caucasus, and emeralds were discovered among the mountains. He sent a fleet of wheat ships to Italy, and the price of grain doubled while it was on the way. He sought political favor with the emperor, and was rewarded with the governorship of the city.

The beauty of Athenais lost nothing with the passing seasons, but grew more perfect, even under the inexplicable shade of dissatisfaction that sometimes veiled it. "Fair as the wife of Hermas" was a proverb in Antioch; and soon men began to add to it, "Beautiful as the son of Hermas." At nine years of age he was straight and strong, firm of limb and clear of eye. His brown head was on a level with his father's heart.

That year another drop of success fell into Hermas' brimming cup. His black Numidian horses, which he had been training for the world-renowned chariot races of Antioch, won the victory over a score of rivals. Hermas received the prize carelessly from the judge's hands, and turned to drive once more around the circus. He paused to lift his son into the chariot beside him to share his triumph.

Here, indeed, was the glory of his life—this matchless son touching his arm, and balancing himself proudly on the swaying floor of the chariot. As the horses pranced around the ring, a great shout of applause filled the amphitheatre, and thousands of spectators waved their salutations of praise: "Hail, fortunate Hermas, master of success! Hail, little Hermas, prince of good luck!"

The sudden tempest of acclamation startled the horses. They dashed violently forward, and plunged upon the bits. The left rein broke. They swerved to the right, swinging the chariot sideways with a grating noise, and dashing it against the stone parapet of the arena. In an instant the wheel was shattered. The axle struck the ground, and the chariot was dragged onward, rocking and staggering.

By a strenuous effort Hermas kept his place on the frail platform, clinging to the unbroken rein. But the boy was tossed lightly from his side at the first shock. His head struck the wall. And when Hermas turned to look for him, he was lying like a broken flower on the sand.

They carried the boy in a litter to the House of the Golden Pillars, summoning the most skillful physician of Antioch to attend him. For hours the child was as quiet as death. Hermas watched the white eyelids, folded closed like lily-buds at night, even as one watches for the morning. At last they opened; but the fire of fever was burning in the eyes, and the lips were moving in a wild delirium.

Hermas was like a man in a nightmare. He paced to and fro, now hurrying to the boy's bed as if he could not bear to be away from it, now turning back as if he could not endure to be near it. The people of the house, even Athenais, feared to speak to him; there was something so vacant and desperate in his face.

At nightfall on the second of those eternal days Hermas shut himself in the library. He sank into a chair like a man in whom the very spring of being is broken. Through the darkness someone drew near. He did not even lift his head. A hand touched him; a soft arm was laid over his shoulders. It was Athenais, kneeling beside him and speaking very low:

"Hermas—it is almost over—the child! His voice grows weaker hour by hour. He moans and calls for someone to help him; then he laughs. It breaks my heart. He has just fallen asleep. Unless a change comes he cannot last till sunrise. Is there nothing we can do? Is there no power that can save him? Is there no one to pity us and spare us? Let us call, let us beg for compassion and help; let us pray for his life!"

Yes; this was what he wanted—this was the only thing that could bring relief: to pray; to pour out his sorrow somewhere; to find a greater strength than his own and cling to it and plead for mercy and help. How could he let his boy suffer and die, without an effort, a cry, a prayer?

He sank on his knees beside Athenais.

"Out of the depths—out of the depths we call for pity. The light of our eyes is fading—the child is dying. Please spare the child's life, thou merciful...."

Not a word; only that deathly blank. Hermas' heart was like a lump of ice in his bosom. He rose slowly to his feet, lifting Athenais with him.

"It is in vain," he said; "there is nothing for us to do. Long ago I knew something. I think it would have helped us. But I have forgotten it. It is all gone. But I would give all that I have, if I could bring it back again now, at this hour, in this time of our bitter trouble."

A slave entered the room while he was speaking, and approached hesitatingly.

"Master," he said, "John of Antioch, whom we were forbidden to admit to the house, has come again. He would take no denial. Even now he waits in the peristyle; and the old man Marcion is with him, seeking to turn him away."

"Come," said Hermas to his wife, "let us go to him."

In the central hall the two men were standing; Marcion, with disdainful eyes and sneering lips, taunting the unbidden guest; John, silent, quiet, patient, while the wondering slaves looked on in dismay. He lifted his searching gaze to the haggard face of Hermas.

"My son, I knew that I should see you again, even though you did not send for me. I have come to you because I have heard that you are in trouble."

"It is true," answered Hermas, "we are in trouble, desperate trouble. Our child is dying. In all this house, in all the world, there is no one who can help us. I knew something long ago, when I was with you—a word, a name—in which we might have found hope. But I have lost it. I gave it to this man. He has taken it away from me forever."

He pointed to Marcion. The old man's lips curled scornfully. "A word, a name!" he sneered. "What is that, O most wise man and holy Presbyter? A thing of air, a thing that men make to describe their own dreams and fancies. Besides, the young man parted with it of his own free will. He bargained with me. I promised him wealth and pleasure and fame. What did he give in return? An empty name...."

"Servant of demons, be still!" John's voice rang clear, like a trumpet, through the hall." There is a Name which none shall dare to take in vain. There is a Name which none can lose without being lost. There is a Name at which the devils tremble. Go quickly, Marcion, before I speak it!"

Marcion shrank into the shadow of one of the pillars. A lamp near him tottered on its pedestal and fell with a crash. In the confusion he vanished.

John turned to Hermas, and his tone softened as he said: "My son, the word with which you parted so lightly is the key word of all life. Without it the world has no meaning, existence, no peace, death, no refuge. It is the word that purifies love, and comforts grief, and keeps hope alive forever. It is the most precious word that ever ear has heard, or mind has known, or heart has conceived. It is the Name of Him who has given us life and breath and all things richly to enjoy; the Name of Him who, though we may forget Him, never forgets us; the Name of Him who pities us as you pity your suffering child; the Name of Him who, though we wander far from Him, seeks us in the wilderness, and sent His Son, even as His Son has sent me this night, to breathe again that forgotten Name in the heart that is perishing without it. Listen, my son, listen with all your soul to the blessed Name of God our Father."

The cold agony in the breast of Hermas dissolved like a fragment of ice that melts in the summer sea. A sense of sweet release spread through him from head to foot. The lost was found. The dew of peace fell on his parched soul. He stood upright, and lifted his hands high toward heaven.

"Out of the depths have I cried unto Thee, O Lord! O my God, be merciful to me, for my soul trusts in Thee. My God, You have given; take not Your gift away from me, O my God! Spare the life of my child, O God, my Father, my Father!"

A deep hush followed his prayer. "Listen!" whispered Athenais.

Was it an echo? It could not be, for it came again—the voice of his son, clear and low, waking from sleep, and calling: "Father!"

December 4

Hanging of the Green

MANY OF YOUR traditional home decorations can take on special significance when incorporated into the celebration of Christ's birth this Advent season. One especially meaningful way you can commemorate Christ's character with your traditional holiday decor is through the use of evergreen wreaths, boughs, and trees, which are representative of the new and everlasting life found in Christ Jesus.

Pause to reflect upon the gift God gave you in sending His only Son as you decorate your Christmas tree and fill your home with seasonal boughs, garlands, and wreaths. Encourage your family to think of ways they can share God's bountiful promise of everlasting life with those around them.

Heavenly Father,

May the evergreen decorations around our home this season serve as a constant reminder of our everlasting life. Help us to share that life with others. May the things we say and do reflect our hope in Your gift of life. Lord, we thank You that Your gift of everlasting life is not just a quantity of life, but a quality of life as well. Thank You for Your abundant provision.

Father, Your Word says that You know what we have need of, even before we ask. (SEE MATTHEW 6:8.) *But because You want relationship with us, You want us to talk to You like we would a Father, You have told us to ask in faith for the things we need. So as a family today, we lay before You all our needs. [Name your family's specific needs.] We know that You are well able to meet these needs and we ask that they are met in Your timing according to Your will. Only You know the end from the beginning and You know what is best for us. We trust in You. Nothing is impossible for You.* (SEE LUKE 1:37.)

We praise You, Lord, for all the things You've done for us in the past and all You're going to do. You are worthy of our reverence and praise.

Thank You, Father.

Amen

What Is Christmas?

Author Unknown

DUSK DESCENDED on the quiet little town of Williamsburg. It was a beautiful, peaceful winter evening. An artist would have a hard time painting a picture that would do the scene justice. There was a light snow falling as Bob Bradley turned and looked out his study window. This time of year always aroused memories for Bob, both pleasant and bleak, and his mind carried him back to the time when, as a boy of twelve, he reached a crossroad in his life.

As a young child he was very happy; he enjoyed all the normal activities most children participate in. Back then, his mom and dad were typical parents who worked together to make their home an enjoyable haven for the family. That was way back in Bob's memories and they were pleasant memories, easy to recall.

Then there was that dreadful day in July. It was a beautiful, lazy summer day and Bob and his mother had enjoyed a trip to the beach, with picnic lunch, sand castles, and wading. When his mother announced it was time to go he really wasn't ready to head for home yet. She, too, had enjoyed the day, but was anxious to have a nice dinner waiting for her husband. Bob's father was foreman for the State Highway Department, and was kept very busy on the new freeway interchange.

Bob recalled how quickly his mother's mood had changed on the drive home. She had a "premonition," she said, and was worried. At that age Bob had not had many encounters with a woman's intuition, but he knew he didn't like the word or the effect it had on his mother. As they turned the corner of their street the first thing to flash into sight was the police car parked in their driveway. Bob recalled how excited he had been to have a real policeman at his house—wait till he told the kids in the neighborhood. His excitement soon vanished, however, as he watched his mother converse with the officer. Her face changed from a pleasant rosy pink to an ashen color, and then tears cascaded down her cheeks.

Mr. Bradley, the officer had told them, was involved in a very serious accident and had been rushed to the nearest hospital. The policeman had come to take Mrs. Bradley to the hospital. That day was the beginning of a thousand days of loneliness for Bob. His father was paralyzed as a result of the accident, and his mother was kept busy caring for him. To Bob, it seemed that she had no time for him, and when he approached his father for companionship, all he received was bitterness. It wasn't until Bob was older that he realized the hardship and adjustment that his father was trying to live through. Needless to say, Bob turned away from his home to find the attention he craved.

He remembered how great he felt when the "gang" finally decided to accept him as a member. What fun they had had together! They started out innocently enough, with pranks common to boys of his age. But one thing led to another—first the pranks, then on to sneaking a smoke and stealing liquor from unsuspecting parents. That gave the gang courage to try bigger things, and the pranks turned into misdemeanors. The next step was drugs, something to help Bob forget the guilt and emptiness that still haunted him. The drugs also helped the gang screw up the courage to "borrow" that late-model car for a drive to the beach and more fun.

Bob paused in his reverie long enough to contemplate the anxieties he had placed on his parents at that time. He sincerely wished he could take an eraser and wipe out the three years that followed his father's accident.

Once again, Bob returned home to find a police car in his driveway. His pounding heart caused anxiety and fear to surge through his body. As it turned out, Bob's wallet had fallen from his pocket and was found on the floor of the stolen car. That was the beginning of many sessions with juvenile counselors and probation officers. In spite of all that, the need to be accepted and wanted by someone was too great to be denied, and Bob returned again and again to the gang. His mother had reached the breaking point. She was working a part-time job to supplement the compensation they received for his father's accident, but she was overwhelmed. Her capacity for handling problems had been filled, and she was sharp with Bob and lacked the understanding that he needed.

The course Bob had chosen had only one possible hope for a good ending—the juvenile detention home for Bob. How he despised the day the officers took him there! He had never felt more confused, frustrated, and alone. By now, his father was able to manipulate a wheelchair, and he made a pitiful sight as Bob told him good-bye. His mother could not contain her tears. She had failed him, she said. Then came the solicitous Mrs. Miller, matron of the home. "We hope you'll find your stay with us happy." What a joke! To top off his belligerent feeling was the introduction of the other "inmates," as he referred to them from that day on.

Life was about to change drastically for Bob, and he wanted desperately to be left alone to shape his own destiny. The year he spent in the home was a good year—what a problem he presented to them, though! He was behind almost every disaster that racked the home, and there was always "that dumb, freckle-faced Becky" tattling on him.

Bob had learned to accept almost everything that came his way. Almost everything, that is, except playing the part of Joseph in the detention home's Christmas play. What a bum that Joseph was—no spirit of fun at all, and to top it all off, "freckle face" was playing the part of Mary.

Then, as if to really test his patience, Mrs. Miller announced that the night of the Christmas program her six-month-old grandson, Andrew, was to be in the pageant as the child in the manger. Bob could picture it now—right in the middle of the pageant Andy was bound to set up a squall.

What is Christmas anyway? A dream when you are a child—one that shatters with reality. That "Peace on Earth" stuff was a lie!

Finally the big night arrived, and the home was a hive of excitement. As Bob came downstairs to help set up chairs, Mr. Miller called to him, "Bob, I need to talk to you after the program, so please stay downstairs." *Great,* Bob thought, *Becky probably told on me again.*

The crowd started gathering, and soon it was time for the play to begin. As Joseph and Mary started their journey toward Bethlehem, Bob's mind journeyed, too. He couldn't quite buy this Christmas business. What was the matter with people? Joyous time of the year—oh, sure! Then came the scene when that freckle-faced Mary placed the baby in the manger. It wouldn't be long now—Andy would soon be screaming and save all of them from this farce.

Out of disinterested boredom, Bob's eyes fell on the baby, who was looking at him with the biggest blue eyes he had ever seen. Very stealthily, Bob's hand crept toward the baby, and the baby reached out and grasped his fingers. An odd feeling surged though Bob, and suddenly he didn't care if people saw him holding onto the child's hand. But when tears came to his eyes, he's had enough. Christmas turned men into blubbering idiots, he decided.

Before he knew it everyone was singing, "Joy to the World." In utter amazement, he found himself joining in the singing. Then it was over, and people were swarming all over the place. As Bob looked across the room, he picked out the faces of his mother and father in the crowd. His father was now able to walk with the use of a cane. His mother had dressed up for the occasion and looked very beautiful. A lump arose in Bob's throat.

At that moment Mr. Miller approached him. "Come into my study, Bob." *Well, here goes nothing,* Bob thought as he followed him into the study. What followed has always been a blur, and hard for Bob to completely understand. He remembers Mr. Miller telling him he was to return to his parents' home. The Probate Judge had decided it was time for him to leave the home, but Bob was to return two hours every night after school and on Saturdays to help Mr. Miller with various chores. In all honesty, Bob experienced a feeling of despair. He was apprehensive about leaving the home, yet relieved that he could. He yearned for his parents, but yet was frightened of the prospect of facing the unknown.

Years later, Bob had never really left the home; the part-time help with chores had turned into a full-time challenge. His parents were older now but still very close and dear to him. Now it was Christmastime once more. Once again, it was time for the detention home's annual Christmas play. Bob had smiled when fifteen-year-old Monty exclaimed, "You want me to be Joseph? Oh, no! Joseph was a bum!" Now he smiled as he remembered his interpretation of the meaning of Christmas. What was Christmas, anyhow? Christmas is a dream when you are a child, one that can shatter in the teen years, but suddenly when you are older, once more the magic of Christmas is yours. What a special time of year!

At that moment, Bob's reverie was broken by the opening of the study door. "Bob, dear, it's time for the play to start." And as Bob looked up at his wife he once more marveled at how a freckle-faced pest like Becky could ever become so lovely. They walked to the auditorium arm in arm. And it was with genuine understanding that Bob greeted the crowd, "May peace be yours, may happiness dwell in your hearts, and may all of you have a Merry Christmas."

December 5

The Nativity Scene

AS YOU ENDEAVOR to focus on the joy of Christ and His coming this Advent season, you can create a wonderful visual reminder of the story of His birth through the addition of a nativity scene to your home's holiday decor.

Along with your family, read Luke's account of Jesus' birth before you display the figures of your nativity scene this year. Some families enjoy allowing their children to take turns positioning the figures of the nativity each day. Remember to let your nativity scene serve as a daily reminder of Jesus' special birth.

Father God,

We come to You today humbly, like the shepherds, and we thank You for the wonderful gift of Your Son. Thank You for shining Your light in our lives.

Father God, thank You for cleansing our hearts and minds. We want to know You and Your Son more and more each day. Thank You for the Holy Spirit who teaches us and leads us into all truth. (SEE JOHN 16:13.) *May we learn new truths about You each day throughout the Advent season, and not only now, but all year long.*

God, You are worthy of all our praise and adoration. Like Mary, we glorify You and rejoice in You our Savior. You have been so good to us and understand our weaknesses and love us still. You have done great things for us. You are holy. You are merciful and compassionate to all who fear You. You have performed mighty acts in the earth, yet You can number the hairs on our heads. (SEE LUKE 12:7.)

Thank You, Father God, for including us in Your great plan of redemption.

In Jesus' awesome name,

Amen

The Foretelling and Fulfillment of Jesus' Birth

Gabriel Visits Mary—Luke 1:26-38 cev

OD SENT THE angel Gabriel to the town of Nazareth in Galilee with a message for a virgin named Mary. She was engaged to Joseph from the family of King David.

The angel greeted Mary and said, "You are truly blessed! The Lord is with you." Mary was confused by the angel's words and wondered what they meant.

Then the angel told Mary, "Don't be afraid! God is pleased with you, and you will have a son. His name will be Jesus. He will be great and will be called the Son of God Most High. The Lord God will make him king, as his ancestor David was. He will rule the people of Israel forever, and his kingdom will never end."

Mary asked the angel, "How can this happen? I am not married!" The angel answered, "The Holy Spirit will come down to you, and God's power will come over you. So your child will be called the holy Son of God. Your relative Elizabeth is also going to have a son, even though she is old. No one thought she could ever have a baby, but in three months she will have a son. Nothing is impossible for God!"

Mary said, "I am the Lord's servant! Let it happen as you have said." And the angel left her.

Mary Visits Elizabeth [LUKE 1:39-45 CEV]

A short time later Mary hurried to a town in the hill country of Judea. She went into Zechariah's home, where she greeted Elizabeth. When Elizabeth heard Mary's greeting, her baby moved within her. The Holy Spirit came upon Elizabeth. Then in a loud voice she said to Mary: "God has blessed you more than any other woman! He has also blessed the child you will have. Why should the mother of my Lord come to me? As soon as I heard your greeting, my baby became happy and moved within me. The Lord has blessed you because you believed that he will keep his promise."

Mary's Song of Praise [LUKE 1:46-56]

Mary said:

"With all my heart I praise the Lord, and I am glad because of God my Savior. God cares for me, his humble servant. From now on, all people will say God has blessed me.

"God All-Powerful has done great things for me, and his name is holy. He always shows mercy to everyone who worships him. The Lord has used his powerful arm to scatter those who are proud. God drags strong rulers from their thrones and puts humble people in places of power. God gives the hungry good things to eat, and sends the rich away with nothing.

He helps his servant Israel and is always merciful to his people. The Lord made this promise to our ancestors, to Abraham and his family forever!"

Mary stayed with Elizabeth about three months. Then she went back home.

The Birth of John the Baptist [LUKE 1:57-80 CEV]

When Elizabeth's son was born, her neighbors and relatives heard how kind the Lord had been to her, and they too were glad. Eight days later they did for the child what the Law of Moses commands. They were going to name him Zechariah, after his father.

But Elizabeth said, "No! His name is John."

The people argued, "No one in your family has ever been named John." So they motioned to Zechariah to find out what he wanted to name his son. Zechariah asked for a writing tablet. Then he wrote, "His name is John." Everyone was amazed.

Right away, Zechariah started speaking and praising God.

All the neighbors were frightened because of what had happened, and everywhere in the hill country people kept talking about these things. Everyone who heard about this wondered what this child would grow up to be. They knew that the Lord was with him.

The Holy Spirit came upon Zechariah, and he began to speak:

"Praise the Lord, the God of Israel! He has come to save his people. Our God has given us a mighty Savior from the family of David his servant. Long ago the Lord promised by the words of his holy prophets to save us from our enemies and from everyone who hates us. God said he would be kind to our people and keep his sacred promise. He told our ancestor Abraham that he would rescue us from our enemies. Then we could serve him without fear, by being holy and good as long as we live.

"You, my son, will be called a prophet of God in heaven above. You will go ahead of the Lord to get everything ready for him. You will tell his people that they can be saved when their sins are forgiven. God's love and kindness will shine upon us like the sun that rises in the sky. On us who live in the dark shadow of death this light will shine to guide us into a life of peace."

As John grew up, God's Spirit gave him great power. John lived in the desert until the time he was sent to the people of Israel.

An Angel Visits Joseph [MATTHEW 1:18-24 CEV]

This is how Jesus Christ was born. A young woman named Mary was engaged to Joseph from King David's family. But before they were married, she learned that she was going to have a baby by God's Holy Spirit. Joseph was a good man and did not want to embarrass Mary in front of everyone. So he decided to quietly call off the wedding.

While Joseph was thinking about this, an angel from the Lord came to him in a dream. The angel said, "Joseph, the baby that Mary will have is from the Holy Spirit. Go ahead and marry her. Then after her baby is born, name him Jesus, because he will save his people from their sins."

So the Lord's promise came true, just as the prophet had said, "A virgin will have a baby boy, and he will be called Immanuel," which means "God is with us."

After Joseph woke up, he and Mary were soon married, just as the Lord's angel had told him to do.

Jesus Is Born ❧ [LUKE 2:1-7 CEV]

About that time Emperor Augustus gave orders for the names of all the people to be listed in record books. These first records were made when Quirinius was governor of Syria. Everyone had to go to their own hometown to be listed.

So Joseph had to leave Nazareth in Galilee and go to Bethlehem in Judea. Long ago Bethlehem had been King David's hometown, and Joseph went there because he was from David's family. Mary was engaged to Joseph and traveled with him to Bethlehem. She was soon going to have a baby, and while they were there, she gave birth to her first-born son. She dressed him in baby clothes and laid him on a bed of hay, because there was no room for them in the inn.

An Angel Visits the Shepherds ❧ [LUKE 2:8-20 CEV]

That night in the fields near Bethlehem some shepherds were guarding their sheep. All at once an angel came down to them from the Lord, and the brightness of the Lord's glory flashed around them. The shepherds were frightened. But the angel said,

"Don't be afraid! I have good news for you, which will make everyone happy. This very day in King David's hometown a Savior was born for you. He is Christ the Lord. You will know who he is, because you will find him dressed in baby clothes and lying on a bed of hay."

Suddenly many other angels came down from heaven and joined in praising God. They said: "Praise God in heaven! Peace on earth to everyone who pleases God." After the angels had left and gone back to heaven, the shepherds said to each other, "Let's go to Bethlehem and see what the Lord has told us about." They hurried off and found Mary and Joseph, and they saw the baby lying on a bed of hay. When the shepherds saw Jesus, they told his parents what the angel had said about him. Everyone listened and was surprised.

But Mary kept thinking about all this and wondering what it meant.

As the shepherds returned to their sheep, they were praising God and saying wonderful things about him. Everything they had seen and heard was just as the angel had said.

Simeon Sees the Savior [LUKE 2:21-40 CEV]

Eight days later Jesus' parents did for him what the Law of Moses commands. And they named him Jesus, just as the angel had told Mary when he promised she would have a baby. The time came for Mary and Joseph to do what the Law of Moses says a mother is supposed to do after her baby is born. They took Jesus to the temple in Jerusalem and presented him to the

Lord, just as the Law of the Lord says, "Each first-born baby boy belongs to the Lord."

The Law of the Lord also says that parents have to offer a sacrifice, giving at least a pair of doves or two young pigeons. So that is what Mary and Joseph did.

At this time a man named Simeon was living in Jerusalem. Simeon was a good man. He loved God and was waiting for God to save the people of Israel. God's Spirit came to him and told him that he would not die until he had seen Christ the Lord.

When Mary and Joseph brought Jesus to the temple to do what the Law of Moses says should be done for a new baby, the Spirit told Simeon to go into the temple.

Simeon took the baby Jesus in his arms and praised God, "Lord, I am your servant, and now I can die in peace, because you have kept your promise to me. With my own eyes I have seen what you have done to save your people, and foreign nations will also see this. Your mighty power is a light for all nations, and it will bring honor to your people Israel."

Jesus' parents were surprised at what Simeon had said.

Then he blessed them and told Mary, "This child of yours will cause many people in Israel to fall and others to stand. The child will be like a warning sign. Many people will reject him, and you, Mary, will suffer as though you had been stabbed by a dagger. But all this will show what people are really thinking."

The prophet Anna was also there in the temple. She was the daughter of Phanuel from the tribe of Asher, and she was very old. In her youth she had been married for seven years, but her husband died. And now she was eighty-four years old. Night and day she served God in the temple by praying and often going without eating. At that time Anna came in and praised God. She spoke about the child Jesus to everyone who hoped for Jerusalem to be set free.

After Joseph and Mary had done everything that the Law of the Lord commands, they returned home to Nazareth in Galilee. The child Jesus grew. He became strong and wise, and God blessed him.

December 6

The Jesse Tree

THE BIRTH OF Jesus Christ from the family of Jesse was the fulfillment of God's promise to His people, both before and since. You can join in the celebration of this beautiful fulfilled promise by enjoying one of the most beloved and widespread traditions of the Advent season.

Decorate a "Jesse Tree" made from a bare branch, a potted house plant, or a small Christmas tree with symbols of those who prepared the way for Christ (i.e., David's harp, Joseph's coat, etc.). Be creative as you fashion your own original and heartfelt version of the "Jesse Tree." Your "Jesse Tree" will serve as a poignant reminder of God's great love as you celebrate the birth of His Son this Advent season.

Heavenly Father,

Thank You for the gift of Your Word. Thank You for the stories of the Old Testament that were given for our instruction and understanding. We can learn many things from those great heroes of the faith who heard Your voice, listened to Your call, and obeyed Your commands.

Like Noah, may we hear Your voice and obey You even if what You're telling us to do seems crazy. Let us be like Abraham, whom You called Your friend. (SEE JAMES 2:23.) *He never quit believing in Your promises, even when he didn't see how they would come to pass. May we learn from Moses to follow You, even if we have to forsake the things we know and do things we don't think we can do. And like David, may we be a family of people who are after Your own heart. May our souls long for You and find You in everything we do.*

Thank You, Lord.

Amen ⁂

A Civil War Fir Tree

Author Unknown

BACK DURING THE Civil War, a mother lived with her two children in a small cottage and struggled to survive such troubled times. The boy, Jacob, was eight years old, and the little girl, Melissa, was six. They longed for their father, who had been away for over a year, fighting in the war. The family was very poor, for soldiers from both armies had taken their farm animals and most of their other food, too. They survived on the kindness of their neighbors, who weren't much better off themselves. That's often how life is—those with little to give are the most generous.

Now wars are hard on people, but they're hard on forests too. All the woods around Jacob and Melissa's town had been badly hurt by cannon fire and musket fire, and soldiers cutting down trees for fires and fortifications. In the woods near their house, a battle had destroyed many of the great old trees, but a very young fir tree had been left standing, untouched, because he was so short the cannonballs had flown quite over his head.

He had been sad to see his elders die such rough deaths, but it is the fate of all trees to die someday, and many trees long to be useful first, being transformed with human help into houses or boats or fences. The young fir tree dreamt of one day being cut down to be used as a mast for a fighting ship—*what a fine destiny for a tree,* he thought! He imagined the sails that would hang from him, and how, even in the worst storm, he would be dependable and never break, and all the sailors would praise him. But right now he was too little to be a mast, or even to cut for fortifications. And no one wanted him for firewood, since there were so many other trees already lying broken and ready on the forest floor. So he felt rather useless. He despaired that the whole war might finish, and nothing exciting would happen to him.

The weather grew colder, and the tall soldiers who passed the little tree looked hungrier and wearier, and his heart went out to them. But no one noticed him, until one day, a strange woman came to the forest, accompanied by a small boy and a smaller girl, who was bundled up and coughed harshly in the cold. "It's such a little one," said Jacob. "It's all that I can carry on my own," said his mother. And then, to the little tree's utter delight, she used her ax and chopped him down. *What an adventure!* thought the tree. Perhaps she makes boats, and will use me as…well, as a very small mast in a smallish kind of boat.

Jacob and Melissa followed their mother as she dragged the little tree back to their small, but cozy cottage, and placed him upright in the corner inside. *What am I to be,* wondered the little tree. But when they took out their old toys—for they had few decorations—and bits of ribbon, and began to decorate him, he realized that he had become a Christmas tree. Very few families had Christmas trees back then, but the mother and father had come from Germany where Christmas trees were a holiday tradition.

Now, on the one hand, thought the little fir tree, *there is no finer destiny for any tree than to become a Christmas tree, if you're the sort of tree who wants to be transformed into something useful. But on the other hand, he really had wanted to do something exciting and important, with lots of howling wind and crashing waves.* However, it appeared that he had little choice in the matter, he concluded, so he drew himself up as straight and tall as he could, straight as the mast on the finest sailing ship. Then he held out his branches for the toys and decorations, being careful not to drop a single one.

That night, which happened to be Christmas Eve, the mother explained to Jacob and Melissa that she had no money for presents, but they would have a good dinner to eat from food that their neighbors had shared. But Melissa was coughing so much she could hardly eat, and she lay down on the couch after dinner, gazing at the tree, still coughing. Her mother would have summoned a doctor, but all the doctors had left months before to help in the war.

The three sat in the warm glow of the candlelight, and Mother said that even though there were no presents, she could give them stories. So she began telling stories—every story she could think of—family stories, stories from the Bible, fairy tales, and even one ghost story, as Jacob listened and Melissa finally fell asleep. And the little tree listened too and remembered every word, because trees have the best memories of all the plants, far better than the ivy, who remembers only what it wants to, or the grass, which remembers nothing.

The next few days, the family kept the Christmas tree up in the corner of the cottage, but he didn't see Melissa much, for she was in bed sick. The mother looked worried all the time, and he wanted to help her, but all he could do was to hold up the toys and stand straight as a mast. As he stood there, he felt his first needles drop, a kind of itchy feeling but not unpleasant, just part of being a Christmas tree.

The next morning, Jacob and his mother removed the toys from the tree and took him out to the shed. "Don't cut it up yet," said Jacob. "It's such a little tree; it won't do very well for firewood anyway." And the mother agreed, although the family had very little wood left, and she didn't have much time to go chop more. Every possible minute she was at Melissa's side, for the child had developed a fever and chills.

The little fir tree looked around the shed, where he was lying on his side, and met the gaze of a family of mice. "You don't look very good to eat," said the youngest mouse. Even the mice had a hard time during the war, because the grain had been taken away from the houses.

"I don't think I'm the least bit good to eat," agreed the tree, who had never heard of a tree whose destiny was to be eaten by mice. "But I might be rather useful as a house, and my needles—which are falling all over the floor, I see—will make a warm bed for your whole family." The mice thought that a capital idea and they moved right in to the very heart of the tree. That night, the silence broken only by a shutter banging in the wind, the youngest mouse couldn't sleep because he was so hungry. "I can't give you food," the little tree told him, "but I can tell you the best stories anyone ever heard." And so the tree told him all the stories he had heard Jacob and Melissa's mother tell, until the mouse fell asleep on the little tree's needles, and snored a tiny mouse snore. Soon the little tree fell asleep too, because he was drying out, which made him very drowsy.

Two days later, all the wood in the shed had been used up. "They'll burn you next," said the father mouse, warningly.

"Do you think so?" said the tree, who was half asleep all the time now. "How exciting! I'll do my best to make a great fire, if only I can stay awake." And soon, the mother came in with an ax and cut the little tree up into pieces.

Using the pieces of the little tree, she built a great fire and brought Melissa near to it. "If only the fever will break," she said. And the little fir tree, who was not sure if he was dreaming or awake—plus there were so many pieces of him now—burned as hot as he could as long as he could, all through the night, keeping Melissa warm.

The next day, when Melissa's mother rose to check on her, the fever was gone, and even her cough was better. In the fireplace, nothing was left—not even a morsel—of the little fir tree. He had burned himself into ashes, until he was just a dream of a Christmas tree, and a new story for the children to tell on future Christmas Eves.

December 7

The Advent Candle

THE BOOK OF John tells us that Jesus came as the "light of the world." Place an Advent candle in a window of your home as a remembrance for yourself and others of this important truth. Modern-day electric candles can be purchased at many stores and are a practical and safe alternative to real wax candles.

A candle placed in the window has a dual symbolism in Europe over centuries past, where wayfarers were welcomed by its light. Each time you see the Advent candle in your window, take time to reflect on your special responsibility as a Christian to be a carrier of the light of Jesus to the lost world around you.

Father God,

Thank You for sending us the light. Jesus is the light of the world and we thank You that if we walk in His light we can have fellowship with one another and Jesus' blood will cleanse us and purify us from all sin. (1 JOHN 1:7.) *Thank You for the purity that we can walk in because of Your light. Thank You that You made the Light of the World shine in our hearts to give us the light of knowledge of the glory of God in the face of Christ.* (2 CORINTHIANS 4:6.)

The Psalmist prayed often for Your light to illuminate his life. With David, we pray that You keep our lamp burning and turn our darkness into light. (PSALM 18:28.) *You are our light and salvation—whom will we fear? You are the stronghold of our lives—whom will we be afraid of?* (PSALM 27:1.) *No one! We fear only You, Lord, for the fear of the Lord is the beginning of wisdom.* (PROVERBS 1:7.)

Lord, send us Your light and Your truth. May they guide us to those who need them. Let our lights shine in the darkness and bring hope and healing to those who need it. May we shine the light of Your love and truth on those in need, and in so doing, glorify You and lift You up so that the whole world can see by Your light.

In Jesus' name,

Amen ❀

Papa Panov's Special Christmas

By Leo Tolstoy

I T WAS CHRISTMAS Eve and although it was still afternoon, lights had begun to appear in the shops and houses of the little Russian village, for the short winter day was nearly over. Excited children scurried indoors and now only muffled sounds of chatter and laughter escaped from closed shutters.

Old Papa Panov, the village shoemaker, stepped outside his shop to take one last look around. The sounds of happiness, the bright lights, and the faint but delicious smells of Christmas cooking reminded him of past Christmases when his wife had still been alive and his own children little. Now they had gone. His usually cheerful face, with the little laughter wrinkles behind the round steel spectacles, looked sad now. But he went back indoors with a firm step, put up the shutters, and set a pot of coffee to heat on the charcoal stove. Then, with a sigh, he settled in his big armchair.

Papa Panov did not often read, but tonight he pulled down the big old family Bible and, slowly tracing the lines with one forefinger, he read again the Christmas story. He read how Mary and Joseph, tired by their journey to Bethlehem, found no room for them at the inn, so that Mary's little baby was born in the cowshed.

"Oh, dear, oh, dear!" exclaimed Papa Panov, "if only they had come here! I would have given them my bed and I could have covered the baby with my patch-work quilt to keep him warm."

He read on about the wise men who had come to see the baby Jesus, bringing Him splendid gifts. Papa Panov's face fell. *I have no gift that I could give Him,* he thought sadly.

Then his face brightened. He put down the Bible, got up and stretched his long arms toward the shelf high up in his little room. He took down a small, dusty box and opened it. Inside was a perfect pair of tiny leather shoes. Papa Panov smiled with satisfaction. Yes, they were as good as he had remembered— the best shoes he had ever made. "I should give Him those," he decided, as he gently put them away and sat down again.

He was feeling tired now, and the further he read the sleepier he became. The print began to dance before his eyes so that he closed them, just for a minute. In no time at all Papa Panov was fast asleep.

And as he slept he had a dream. He dreamed that someone was in his room and he knew at once, as one does in dreams, who the person was. It was Jesus.

"You have been wishing that you could see Me, Papa Panov." He said kindly, "then look for Me tomorrow. It will be Christmas Day and I will visit you. But look carefully, for I shall not tell you who I am."

When at last Papa Panov awoke, the bells were ringing out and a thin light was filtering through the shutters. "Bless my soul!" said Papa Panov. "It's Christmas Day!"

He stood up and stretched himself for he was rather stiff. Then his face filled with happiness as he remembered his dream. This would be a very special Christmas after all, for Jesus was coming to visit him. How would He look? Would He be a little baby, as at that first Christmas? Would He be a grown man, a carpenter—or the great King that He is, God's Son? He must watch carefully the whole day through so that he would recognize Him however He came.

Papa Panov put on a special pot of coffee for his Christmas breakfast, took down the shutters, and looked out the window. The street was deserted, no one was stirring yet. No one except the road sweeper. He looked as miserable and dirty as ever and well he might! Whoever wanted to work on Christmas Day—and in the raw cold and bitter freezing mist of such a morning?

Papa Panov opened the shop door, letting in a thin stream of cold air. "Come in!" he shouted across the street cheerily. "Come in and have some hot coffee to keep out the cold!"

The sweeper looked up, scarcely able to believe his ears. He was only too glad to put down his broom and come into the warm room. His old clothes steamed gently in the heat of the stove and he clasped both red hands round the comforting warm mug as he drank.

Papa Panov watched him with satisfaction, but every now and then his eyes strayed to the window. It would never do to miss his special visitor.

"Expecting someone?" the sweeper asked at last. So Papa Panov told him about his dream.

"Well, I hope He comes," the sweeper said. "You've given me a bit of Christmas cheer I never expected to have. I'd say you deserve to have your dream come true." And he actually smiled.

When he had gone, Papa Panov put on cabbage soup for his dinner, and then went to the door again, scanning the street. He saw no one. But he was mistaken. Someone was coming.

The girl walked so slowly and quietly, hugging the walls of shops and houses, that it was a while before he noticed her. She looked very tired and she was carrying something. As she drew nearer he could see that it was a baby, wrapped in a thin shawl. There was such sadness in her face and in the pinched little face of the baby that Papa Panov's heart went out to them.

"Won't you come in" he called, stepping outside to meet them. "You both need a warm rest by the fire."

The young mother let him shepherd her indoors and to the comfort of the armchair. As she sat down, she breathed a big sigh of relief.

"I'll warm some milk for the baby," Papa Panov said, "I've had children of my own—I can feed her for you." He took the milk from the stove and carefully fed the baby from a spoon, warming her tiny feet by the stove at the same time.

"She needs shoes," the cobbler said.

"But I can't afford shoes," the girl replied. "I've got no husband to bring home money. I'm on my way to the next village to get work."

A sudden thought flashed through Papa Panov's mind. He remembered the little shoes he had looked at last night. But he had been keeping those for Jesus. He looked again at the cold little feet and made up his mind.

"Try these on her," he said, handing the baby and the shoes to the mother. The beautiful little shoes were a perfect fit. The girl smiled happily and the baby gurgled with pleasure.

"You have been so kind to us," the girl said, when she got up with her baby to go. "May all your Christmas wishes come true!"

But Papa Panov was beginning to wonder if his very special Christmas wish would come true. Perhaps he had missed his visitor? He looked anxiously up and down the street. There were plenty of people about but they were all faces that he recognized. There were neighbors going to call on their families. They nodded and smiled and wished him Happy Christmas! Or beggars—and Papa Panov hurried indoors to fetch them hot soup and a generous hunk of bread, hurrying out again in case he missed the Important Stranger.

All too soon the winter dusk fell. When Papa Panov next went to the door and strained his eyes, he could no longer make out the passersby. Most everyone was home and indoors by now anyway. He walked slowly back into his room at last, put up the shutters, and sat down wearily in his armchair.

So it had been just a dream after all. Jesus had not come.

Then all at once he knew that he was no longer alone in the room.

This was not a dream for he was wide awake. At first he seemed to see before his eyes the long stream of people who had come to him that day. He saw again the old road sweeper, the young mother and her baby, and the beggars he had fed. As they passed, each whispered, "Didn't you see Me, Papa Panov?"

"Who are You?" he called out, bewildered.

Then another voice answered him. It was the voice from his dream—the voice of Jesus.

"I was hungry and you fed Me," he said. "I was naked and you clothed Me. I was cold and you warmed Me. I came to you today in every one of those you helped and welcomed."

Then all was quiet and still. The only sound was the ticking of the big clock. A great peace and happiness seemed to fill the room, overflowing Papa Panov's heart until he wanted to burst out singing and laughing and dancing with joy.

"So he did come after all!" was all that he said.

December 8

The Blessing Box

REMIND YOUR FAMILY of how blessed they are this Advent season by creating a personalized blessing box to be given to an individual or family in need.

A blessing box can be made by decorating a small, empty box and placing it in a central location in your home. Offerings of money or other special items should be added to the box daily as family members join together to share accounts of their own blessings—perhaps at family dinner each night. As Christmas Day nears, pass along the fruit of your thankful hearts to someone who desperately needs it. In doing so, your family will be blessed beyond measure and filled with the true joy of the Advent season.

Father God,

You are the ultimate Giver. Let us approach this season of Advent with gratitude in our hearts for all of Your wonderful gifts. May we learn to give generously and selflessly to those around us. As You have blessed us, may we learn to bless others.

You are our great Provider, Father God. We praise You for Your loving care for our family and thank You for opportunities to share with those we come in contact with each day. Your Word says that we are Your sheep and we hear Your voice. (JOHN 10:27.) Thank You for speaking to our hearts about who we should give to and what we should give.

We pray that the needs of those around us would be met with Your abundant provision. Thank You, Father God, that You care about even the smallest needs and desires we have. We pray that even the small things our friends and family—and even our enemies—are hoping for this holiday season, will be given to them in Your perfect timing. Lord, thank You for Your abundant grace and mercy.

In Jesus' name,

Amen

An Exchange of Gifts

Author Unknown

O MARION, CHRISTMAS had always been a time of enchantment, but never more so than the year when her son Marty was eight. That was the year she and her children moved into a cozy trailer home in the woods just outside of Cheyenne, Oklahoma.

As the holidays approached, Marion's spirit was light, unhampered even by the winter rains that swept across the Oklahoma hills, dousing their home and making the floors muddy. Throughout that December, Marty had been the most spirited and busiest of them all. He was the youngest; a cheerful boy, blond-haired and playful, with a quaint habit of looking up at you and cocking his head like a puppy when you talked to him. Actually, the reason for this was that Marty was deaf in his left ear, but he never once complained about it.

Marion had been watching Marty curiously for weeks. She could tell that something was going on with him. Every day, Marty eagerly made his bed, took out the trash, carefully set the table, and helped his older brother and sister prepare dinner before their mom came from work. Every week, he quietly collected his tiny allowance and tucked it away, not spending a cent of it.

Marion had no idea what all this was about, but she suspected that somehow it had something to do with Kenny. Kenny was Marty's best friend, and ever since they had found each other last spring, they were seldom apart. If you called to one, you got them both. Their world was in a meadow, a pasture broken by a small winding stream, where they caught frogs and snakes, searched for arrowheads or hidden treasure, and spent the afternoon feeding squirrels peanuts.

Times were hard for Marion's little family, but with a lot of ingenuity, scrimping, and saving, they were much better off than Kenny's family. His family was desperately poor, and his mother struggled to feed and clothe Kenny and his little sister. They were a good, solid family. But Kenny's mom was a proud woman, very proud, and she had strict rules.

How they worked, as they did each year, to make their home festive for the holiday! Marty and Kenny would sometimes sit still at the table long enough to help make cornucopias or weave little baskets for the Christmas tree. But before long, one would whisper to the other, and they'd be out the door and sliding cautiously under the electric fence into the horse pasture that separated Marty's home from Kenny's.

One night, shortly before Christmas, when Marion's hands were deep in cookie dough, Marty went to her and said in a tone mixed with pleasure and pride, "Mom, I've bought Kenny a Christmas present. Want to see it?" *So that's what he's been up to*, she said to herself. "It's something he's wanted for a long, long time, Mom." After carefully wiping his hands on a dish towel, he pulled a small box from his pocket. When he lifted the lid, Marion gazed at the pocket compass that her son had been saving all those allowances to buy. A little compass to point an eight-year-old adventurer through the woods.

"It's a lovely gift, Martin," she said, but even as she spoke, a disturbing thought came to mind: She knew how Kenny's mother felt about their poverty. They could barely afford to exchange gifts among themselves, and giving presents to others was out of the question. Marion was sure that Kenny's proud mother would not permit her son to receive something that he could not return in kind. Very gently and carefully, she talked over the problem with Marty. He understood what she was saying. "I know, Mom, I know! But what if it was a secret? What if they never found out who gave it?" She didn't know how to answer him. She just wasn't sure what would happen.

The day before Christmas was rainy and cold and gray. Marion and the three kids all but fell over one another as they elbowed their way about their little home, putting finishing touches on Christmas secrets and preparing for family and friends who would be dropping by. Night came, and the rain continued. Marion looked out the window over the sink and felt an odd sadness. How mundane the rain seemed for a Christmas Eve! It seemed to her that strange and wonderful things happened only on clear nights, nights when one could at least see a single star in the heavens.

She turned from the window lost in her thoughts, and as she checked on the ham and bread warming in the oven, she saw Marty slip out the door. He wore his coat over his pajamas, and he clutched a tiny, colorfully wrapped box in his hand. Down through the soggy pasture he went, then a quick slide under the electric fence and across the yard to Kenny's house. Up the steps on tiptoe, shoes squishing, he opened the screen door just a crack; placed the gift on the doorstep, took a deep breath, reached for the doorbell, and pressed on it hard.

Quickly, Marty turned and ran down the steps and across the yard trying to get away unnoticed. Then, suddenly, he ran straight into the electric fence. The shock sent him reeling. He lay stunned on the wet ground. His body quivered and he gasped for breath. Then slowly, Marty began the grueling trip back home. "Marty," Marion cried as he stumbled through the door, "what happened?" His lower lip quivered, his eyes brimmed over with tears. "I forgot about the fence, and it knocked me down!" Marion hugged Marty's muddy little body to herself. He was still dazed and there was a red mark blistering on his face from his mouth to his ear. She quickly treated the blister and, with a warm cup of cocoa, Marty's bright spirits returned. Marion tucked him into bed and just before he fell asleep, he looked up at her and said, "Mom, Kenny didn't see me. I'm sure he didn't see me."

That Christmas Eve, Marion went to bed unhappy and puzzled. It seemed such a cruel thing to happen to a little boy on the purest kind of Christmas mission. She did not sleep well that night. Somewhere deep inside she was feeling the disappointment that the night of Christmas had come and it had been just an ordinary, problem-filled night—no mysterious enchantment at all. However, she was wrong.

By morning the rain had stopped and the sun was shining. The streak on Marty's face was very red, but the burn didn't look serious. They opened their presents, and soon Kenny was knocking on the door, eager to show Marty his new compass and tell him about the mystery of its arrival. It was obvious that Kenny didn't suspect Marty at all, and while the two of them talked, Marty just smiled and smiled. As Marion watched the two boys, smiling to herself, she suddenly noticed that while they were chattering away about their Christmases, Marty was not cocking his head. While Kenny was talking, Marty seemed to be listening with his deaf ear.

Weeks later, Marty brought home a report from the school nurse, verifying what Marion and he already knew: "Marty now has complete hearing in both ears." The mystery of exactly how Marty regained his hearing, and still has it, remains just that, a mystery. Doctors suspect, of course, that the shock from the electric fence was somehow responsible. Perhaps so. Whatever the reason, Marion was simply thankful to God for the good exchange of gifts made that night.

Strange and wonderful things still happen on the night of our Lord's birth, she realized. *And one does not have to have a clear night, to follow a fabulous star.*

December 9

The Chrismon Tree

DECORATING YOUR CHRISTMAS tree each year is a beloved tradition enjoyed in homes around the world. You can give your tree special significance this season by making it a "Chrismon Tree."

The word "Chrismon" is a combination of the words "Christ" and "monogram." Create your own "Chrismon Tree" by decorating your Christmas tree with monograms (symbols) of Jesus Christ. Some ideas include the five-pointed star, reminding us of the star that announced the birth of Christ, and the triangle, which is symbolic of the Trinity. "Chrismons" can easily be made using cardstock, glue, markers, and other standard crafting supplies. Be creative as you research symbols to use for your own tree. These special symbols—used alone or along with your traditional tree decorations—will help center your focus on the true importance of Christ's coming in this season of Advent.

Heavenly Father,

We thank You for giving us physical symbols that can remind us of spiritual truths. Thank You for the star that announced the birth of Jesus Christ, and led the shepherds, and later the wise men, to meet the newborn King.

Thank You for the triangle that represents the Trinity—Father, Son, and Holy Spirit. Thank You that it reminds us that You are our Father, Jesus is our brother, Your only begotten Son, and our Redeemer, and the Holy Spirit is our Comforter, who comforts us in all our troubles and leads us into Your truth.

Thank You for the crown that reminds us of the Kingship of Jesus and His victory over sin and death on our behalf. Thank You for the cross, which reminds us of Jesus' death, burial, and resurrection.

Thank You for the symbol of the dove, that reminds us of the Holy Spirit, and how He descended upon Jesus and declared that He was Your beloved Son, in whom you were well pleased. (MATTHEW 3:17.) *Thank You for the butterfly, that reminds us that You have made us new creatures in Christ.* (2 CORINTHIANS 5:17.)

Thank You, Father God, for all these meaningful symbols and more that help us to remember Your great love toward us.

In Jesus' name,

Amen ⁂

The Fir Tree

By Hans Christian Andersen

ANICE LITTLE FIR tree stood out in the woods. The sun shone on him and he had plenty of fresh air. Many large comrades grew around him, pines as well as firs. But the little Fir wanted so very much to be a grown-up tree he did not think of the warm sun and of the fresh air. He did not care for the little children who often came and sat down near the young tree and said, "Oh, how pretty he is! What a nice little fir!" This was what the Tree could not bear to hear.

At the end of a year he had shot up a good deal, and after another year he was another long bit taller. "Oh, if only I were as high a tree as the others!" he sighed. "Then I should be able to spread out my branches, and look into the wide world!" Neither the sunbeams, nor the birds, nor the clouds, which morning and evening sailed above them, gave the little Tree any pleasure.

In winter, when the snow lay glittering on the ground a hare would often come leaping along and jump right over the little Tree. Oh, that made him so angry! But now two winters were past, and in the third the little tree was large enough that the hare was obliged to go round it. *To grow and grow, to get older and be tall,* thought the little Tree—*that, after all, is the most delightful thing in the world!*

In autumn the woodcutters always came and felled some of the largest trees. The young Fir tree had now grown to a very comely size and he trembled at the sight. The magnificent trees fell to the earth with a loud cracking and the branches were lopped off. Then they were laid in carts and the horses dragged them out of the woods. *Where did they go to? What became of them?*

In spring, when the Swallows and the Storks came, the Tree asked them, "Do you know where they have been taken? Have you met them anywhere?" The Swallows didn't know anything about it, but the Stork nodded his head and said: "Yes, I think I know. I met many ships as I was flying hither from Egypt. There were magnificent masts on the ships and I venture to say that they smelt of fir. I may congratulate you, for they lifted themselves on high most majestically!"

"Oh, if only I were old enough to fly across the sea!"

When Christmas came, quite young trees were cut down, trees which often were not even as large as this Fir tree, who could never rest, but always wanted to be off. These young trees, and they were always the finest looking, retained their branches. They too, were laid on carts and the horses drew them out of the woods.

"Where are they going to?" asked the Fir. "They are not taller than I. There was one indeed that was considerably shorter. And why do they retain all their branches? Where are they taken?"

"We know! We know!" chirped the Sparrows. "We have peeped in at the windows in the town below! The greatest splendor and magnificence one can imagine await them. We saw them planted in the middle of a warm room, and ornamented with the most splendid things—gilded apples, gingerbread, toys, and many hundred lights!"

"And then?" asked the Fir tree, trembling in every bough. "And then? What happens then?"

"We did not see anything more. It was incomparably beautiful."

"I would fain know if I am destined for so glorious a career," cried the Tree. "That is better than to cross the sea! Oh, I wish I were already on the cart going to the warm room with all the splendor and magnificence! Yes, then something better, something still grander, will surely follow—but what?"

The Fir tree grew and grew and was green both winter and summer. People that saw him said, "What a fine tree!" And the next Christmas he was one of the first to be cut down. The axe struck deep into his trunk and he fell to the earth with a sigh. His departure was not all that agreeable.

The Tree only came to himself when he was unloaded in a courtyard with the other trees, and heard a man say, "That one is splendid!" Then two servants came in rich livery and carried the Fir tree into a large and splendid drawing room. The Tree was stuck upright in a cask that was filled with sand but no one could see that it was just a cask, for green cloth was hung all around it, and it stood on a large gaily colored carpet. Oh, how the Tree quivered! *What was to happen?*

The servants and the young ladies decorated it. In one branch there hung little nets cut out of colored paper, and each net was filled with sugarplums. Among the other boughs gilded apples and walnuts were suspended, looking as though they had grown there, and little blue and white tapers were placed among the leaves. And at the very top a large star of gold tinsel was fixed. It was truly splendid.

"This evening!" said they all. "How it will shine this evening!"

Oh, thought the Tree, *if the evening were but come! If the tapers were but lighted! And then I wonder what will happen! Perhaps the other trees from the forest will come to look at me! I wonder if I shall take root here, and winter and summer stand covered with ornaments!*

When the candles were finally lighted the Tree trembled so in every bough that one of the tapers set fire to the foliage. It blazed up splendidly. "Help! Help!" cried the young ladies, and they quickly put out the fire.

Now the Tree did not even dare tremble. What a state he was in! He was so uneasy lest he should lose something of his splendor that he was quite bewildered. Suddenly a troop of children rushed in as if they would upset the Tree. The older persons followed quietly and the little ones stood quite still. But only for a moment. Then they shouted so that the whole place echoed with their rejoicing. They danced round the tree and one present after the other was pulled off.

What are they about? thought the Tree. *What is to happen now?* And the lights burned down to the very branches and as they burned down they were put out, one after the other, and then the children had permission to plunder the tree. So they fell upon it with such violence that all its branches cracked. If it had not been fixed firmly in the cask, it would certainly have tumbled down.

The children danced about with their beautiful playthings and no one looked at the Tree except the old nurse, who peeped between the branches but only to see if there was a fig or an apple left that had been forgotten. "A story! a story!" cried the children, drawing a little fat man toward the tree. He seated himself under it and said: "Now we are in the shade, and the Tree can listen, too. But I shall tell only one story."

And the man told about Klumpy-Dumpy that tumbled down, who notwithstanding came to the throne, and at last married the princess. And the children clapped their hands, and cried out, "Oh, go on! Do go on!" The Fir tree stood quite still and absorbed in thought. *Klumpy-Dumpy fell downstairs, and yet he married the princess! Yes! Yes! That's the way of the world!* thought the Fir tree. *Who knows? Perhaps I may fall downstairs, too, and get a princess as a wife!* And he looked forward with joy to the morrow, when he hoped to be decked out again with lights, playthings, fruits, and tinsel.

I won't tremble tomorrow, thought the Fir tree. *I will enjoy all my splendor to the full.* And the whole night the Tree stood still and in deep thought. In the morning the servant and the housemaid came in. *Now, then, the splendor will begin again,* thought the Fir. But they dragged him out of the room and up the stairs into the loft, and there in a dark corner, where no daylight could enter, they left him.

What's the meaning of this? thought the Tree. *What am I to do here?* And he leaned against the wall, lost in thought. Time enough had he, too, for days and nights passed and nobody came up. When at last somebody did come, it was only to put some great trunks away. There stood the Fir tree quite hidden. It seemed as if he had been entirely forgotten.

'Tis now winter out of doors! thought the Tree. *The earth is hard and covered with snow. Men cannot plant me now, and therefore I have been put up here under shelter till the springtime comes! If only it were not so dark here, and so terribly lonely! Not even a hare. And out in the woods it was so pleasant when the snow was on the ground, and the hare leaped by. Yes—even when he jumped over me.*

"Squeak! squeak!" said a little mouse at the same moment, peeping out of his hole. Then out came another one. They sniffed about the Fir tree, and rustled among its branches. "It is dreadfully cold," said the mouse. "But for that, it would be delightful here, old Fir, wouldn't it?"

"I am by no means old," said the Fir tree. "There's many a one considerably older than I am."

"Where do you come from," asked the mice; "and what can you do?" They were extremely curious. "Tell us about the most beautiful spot on the earth. Have you never been there? Were you never in the larder, where cheeses lie on the shelves, and hams hang from above, that place where one enters lean, and comes out again fat and portly?"

"I know no such place," said the Tree, "but I know the woods, where the sun shines, and where the little birds sing." And then he told all about his youth. The little mice had never heard the like before, and they listened and said: "How much you have seen! How happy you must have been!"

"Yes, those were happy times." And then he told about Christmas Eve, when he was decked out with cakes and candles. "Oh," said the little mice, "how fortunate you have been, old Fir tree!"

"I am by no means old," said he. "I came from the woods this winter. I am in my prime, and am only rather short for my age."

"What delightful stories you know!" said the mice. And the next night they came with four other little mice. The more the Fir related the more plainly he remembered it all himself. It appeared as if those times had really been happy times. *But they may still come. Klumpy-Dumpy fell downstairs and yet he got a princess.* And he thought at the moment of a nice little Birch tree growing out in the woods. To the Fir, that would be a charming princess.

"Who is Klumpy-Dumpy?" asked the mice. So the Fir tree told the whole fairy tale, for he could remember every single word. And the little mice jumped for joy. The next night two more mice came, and on Sunday two rats, even. But they said the stories were not interesting, which vexed the little mice; and they, too, now began to think them not so very amusing either.

At last the little mice stayed away and the Tree sighed: "After all, it was very pleasant when the sleek little mice sat around me and listened to what I told them. Now that too is over. But I will take good care to enjoy myself when I am brought out again." But when was that to be?

One morning there came a quantity of people and set to work in the loft. The trunks were moved, the Tree was pulled out and thrown—rather hard, it is true—down on the floor. But a man drew him toward the stairs. *Now a merry life will begin again,* thought the Tree. He felt the fresh air, the first sunbeam—and now he was out in the courtyard. It all passed so quickly, there was so much going on around him that the Tree quite forgot to look to himself. "Now, then, I shall really enjoy life," said he, exultingly, and spread out his branches. But, alas! They were all withered and yellow. He was laid in a corner among weeds and nettles. But he still wore the golden star of tinsel on top, and it glittered in the sunshine.

Some of the merry children who had danced round the Fir tree at Christmas were playing in the courtyard, and were glad at the sight of him. One of the youngest ran and tore off the golden star. "Look what is still on the ugly old Christmas tree!" said he. And the Tree beheld all the beauty of the flowers and the freshness in the garden. He beheld himself and wished he had remained in his dark corner in the loft. He thought of his youth in the woods, of the merry Christmas Eve, and of the little mice who had listened with so much pleasure to the story of Klumpy-Dumpy. "'Tis over—'tis past!" said the poor Tree. "Had I but rejoiced when I had reason to do so! But now 'tis past, 'tis past!"

And the gardener's boy chopped the Tree into small pieces. The wood flamed up splendidly under the large copper pot, and it sighed so deeply! Each sigh was like a shot.

The boys played about in the courtyard and the youngest wore the gold star on his breast which the Tree had worn on the happiest evening of his life. However, that was over now—the Tree gone, the story at an end. Every tale must end at last.

December 10

Lighting the Second Candle
of the Advent Wreath

THE SECOND CANDLE of the Advent wreath is traditionally symbolic of peace. Set aside a special time with your family—perhaps during dinner or family devotions—to reflect on Jesus' role as the Prince of Peace before you light this candle on your Advent wreath.

Together as a family, think of a situation in your lives or the world around you that needs peace. Then pray that God will minister His peace in these situations. Ask the Lord to help you and your family exhibit His peace in your daily lives to all those around you.

Lord,

During the Christmas season the world wishes for Peace on Earth, but we pray that the world would experience Your peace all year long. Jesus is the Prince of Peace and we pray that the world would accept the peace He offers. Thank You that Your peace is true peace, not just a lack of conflict or confusion, but peace in spite of conflict and confusion because we can rest and trust in You.

Thank You, Father God, for Your peace that passes understanding that watches over our hearts and minds. (PHILIPPIANS 4:7.) Thank You that You cause Your beloved to have sweet, peaceful sleep. (PROVERBS 3:24.) We pray that Your peace will rule in our hearts and bring peace to those we come in contact with each day.

We pray for peace in our home, as well as the homes of our family and friends. May their homes be a place of peace and safety, a refuge from the troubles of the world. May we find refreshment and renewal in Your place of peace.

Father God, may our lights shine bright so that others will see it and come to know You and Your peace.

In Jesus' name,

Amen

The Noel Candle

By Clement C. Moore

IT WAS CHRISTMAS Eve in Rheims, France, nearly five hundred years ago. The spires of the great cathedral towered high in the sky over a throng of people who had gathered in the square before the church, celebrating the joyous Noel. Laughing children darted through the crowd as groups of youths and maidens sang carols and danced to the music of a lute and tambourine. Everywhere faces shone with such happiness, it did not seem possible there could be, in all of Rheims, one sad and lonely heart.

Yet there were four. Three of them lived in a squalid old shed by the river. Though its outward appearance was dismal, the inside was neat and clean. Its one room served as living room, dining room, bedroom, and kitchen for three people, but the rough stone floor was carefully swept, and the patched covers on the straw mattresses in the corner were spotlessly clean. A rough table, broken chair, small stool, and rickety bench were the only furniture in the room. In a far corner stood a small charcoal brazier whose weak flame served not only to cook the meals but to warm the hut.

The one touch of beauty in the little room was supplied by a tiny shrine, built on a shelf at the rear wall. A few field flowers in a bowl stood in front of it, and from the shelf hung a heavily embroidered scarlet sash which had once held a knight's shield.

A young woman was bending over a small spinning wheel, a boy of seven was setting the table with their few cracked dishes, and a girl a year or so older was stirring a kettle over the brazier. The lady, whose beauty shone through in spite of her ragged clothing, was Madame la Contesse Marie de Malincourt, and the boy and girl, her son and daughter, Louis and Jeanne.

As she worked, the lady was thinking sadly of Christmas only a year before, when everything had been so different. Then she had lived in a great castle, and as on every Christmas Eve, she and her husband and children had gone down to the castle gate to greet the assembled crowd. The old, the ailing, and the poor would gather there, and the Malincourts would go into the crowd giving each villager gifts of warm clothing, healing herbs, and food. Even Louis and Jeanne would give something from their own toys to the village children.

Then war had swept over their happy valley. Lady Marie's husband had been led away in chains while she and the children fled down a secret passageway out in the night and away to the village. They found it deserted, the villagers frightened away by the attackers.

During the months that followed, the three had wandered along the highway trading away their belongings bit by bit in return for food and lodging. Only one thing remained of their former life—the cover of her husband's shield, which little Louis had brought from the castle that dreadful night. "Father gave it to me to keep until he comes back," he said and through all the terrors of their flight he had clung to it. It was dear to all of them, for it was their only reminder of their father and the life they had shared together.

"Mother," said Jeanne suddenly, interrupting her mother's thoughts, "it is Christmas tonight."

"Yes, sighed Lady Marie, "but there will be no toys or sweets for you and little Louis this Noel."

"We don't need them," the children answered. "We have you, Mother, and we can keep Christmas in our hearts." Their mother looked up at them and smiled. "Yes, though life is hard," she said, "we still have each other, and even though we miss your father, I'm sure there are others in Rheims tonight who miss their loved ones also. I just wish we had something to give the poor as we once did...." A thoughtful silence filled the room.

"Mother," Jeanne said excitedly, "I know something we can give." As she talked she picked up the small tallow candle from the table and hurried to the one window of the hut. "See," she went on, "I will put it on the sill and perhaps someone who passes, someone like us, will be happier because of this little gift of light. There—see how it shines out on the snow?"

"You are a good child, Jeanne," said Lady Marie, and then smiling gently, she resumed her work.

Down in the great square, among all the lights and gaiety, was another sad heart. It beat in the breast of a little lad of nine, a boy in ragged clothes whose bare feet were thrust into clumsy wooden clogs. He was utterly alone in the world, without money or friends—cold, hungry, and miserable. When he tried to tell his story to some of the people milling around him, no one took any interest in him, other than to frown at him or elbow him out of the way. At last, in utter despair, he began to tramp up the streets, stopping now and then to gaze at the splendid houses and to seek help. But there was no welcome in any of them for the poor lonely child.

It was dark in the streets of Rheims now, but the little child trampled on, trying desperately to find shelter before the night closed in. At last, far off down by the river, he saw a tiny gleam of light appear suddenly at a window and he hurried toward it. As he neared it, the boy saw it was only a small tallow candle at the window of a hovel, the poorest hut in all Rheims, but the steady light brought a sudden glow to his heart and he ran forward and knocked at the door.

It was quickly opened by a little girl, and at once two other people had risen to greet him. In another moment he found himself seated on a stool beside the fire. The little girl was warming one of his cold hands in her palms, while her brother was holding the other, and a beautiful woman, kneeling at his feet, drew off the wooden shoes and rubbed his icy feet. When he was thoroughly warmed, the little girl dished the stew which had been simmering on the fire. There was only a little of it, but she passed the fullest bowl to the stranger.

After a word of blessing, they ate their stew, and never had the thick soup tasted so rich and so satisfying. As they finished, a sudden glowing light filled the room, greater than the brightness of a thousand candles. There was a sound of angel voices, and the stranger had grown so radiant they could hardly bear to look at him.

"Thou, with thy little candle, have lighted the Christ child on His way to Heaven," said their guest, his hand on the door latch. "This night your dearest prayer shall be answered," and in another instant he was gone.

The countess and her children fell to their knees and prayed, and there they still were many minutes later when a knight in armor gently pushed open the door and entered the hut.

"Marie! Jeanne! Louis!" he cried. "Don't you know me after all these weary months? How I have searched for you!" Immediately his family clustered around him with embraces and kisses. "But, Father, how did you find us here?" cried little Louis at last. "A ragged lad I met on the highway told me where you live," answered the knight.

"The Christ child," said Marie reverently, and told him the story.

And so, forever after, they and all their descendants have burned a candle in the window on the eve of Noel, to light the solitary Christ child on His way.

December 11

Outdoor Luminaries

DISPLAY YOUR OUTWARD joy at the coming celebration of Christ's birth by using luminaries—special small candles in brown paper bags—to light pathways and driveways during the Advent season.

It is a common custom across much of Mexico and the American Southwest to use luminaries during Advent. You can easily create your own luminaries by filling small brown lunch bags with sand and then adding a votive candle to each. Making your own luminaries for use around your home is a fun family project and a way to remind yourself and others that Jesus is the Word which is a light unto our path.

Heavenly Father,

We thank You for Your Word, that Jesus was the Word and He became flesh and dwelt among us so that we could see the Truth in human form. (JOHN 1:14.) *Thank You for Your Truth that shines in the darkness. Thank You that we can let our lights shine so that others may see our good works and glorify You.* (MATTHEW 5:16.)

Thank You, Father God, that we are Your workmanship. You have made us new creatures in Christ so that we can walk in the good works You have planned for us. (EPHESIANS 2:10.)

Lord, we give our lives to You again. Lead us and guide us in the good works You have planned for our family, and each of us individually. May we see Your face in those we touch this season. Let us see others through Your eyes, through the eyes of love—love that believes the best of every person. May we never become prideful in our giving, but remain humble in our hearts because we know that every good thing we have comes from You. We can do nothing good on our own, it is only through Your grace and mercy that we can give and love and shine Your light in a dark world.

In Jesus' name,

Amen ✾

Bobby Decker's Santa Claus

Author Unknown

I REMEMBER MY first Christmas adventure with Grandma. I was just a kid. I remember tearing across town on my bike to question her on the day my big sister dropped the bomb: "There is no Santa Claus," she jeered. "Even dummies know that!"

My Grandma was not the gushy kind, never had been. I fled to her that day because I knew she would be straight with me. I knew Grandma always told the truth, and I knew that the truth always went down a whole lot easier when swallowed with one of her world-famous cinnamon buns. I knew they were world-famous, because Grandma said so. It had to be true.

Grandma was home, and the buns were still warm. Between bites, I told her everything. She was ready for me. "No Santa Claus!" she snorted. "Ridiculous! Don't believe it. That rumor has been going around for years, and it makes me mad, plain mad. Now, put on your coat, and let's go."

"Go? Go where, Grandma?" I asked. I hadn't even finished my second world-famous cinnamon bun.

"Where" turned out to be Kerby's General Store, the one store in town that had a little bit of just about everything. As we walked through its doors, Grandma handed me ten dollars. That was a bundle in those days. "Take this money," she said, "and buy something for someone who needs it. I'll wait for you in the car." Then she turned and walked out of Kerby's.

I was only eight years old. I'd often gone shopping with my mother, but I had never shopped for anything all by myself. The store seemed big and crowded, full of people scrambling to finish their Christmas shopping. For a few moments I just stood there, confused, clutching that ten-dollar bill, wondering what to buy, and who on earth to buy it for.

I thought of everybody I knew: my family, my friends, my neighbors, the kids at school, the people who went to my church. I was just about thought out, when I suddenly thought of Bobby Decker. He was a kid with bad breath and messy hair, and he sat right behind me in Mrs. Pollock's second grade class. Bobby Decker didn't have a coat. I knew that because he never went out for recess during the winter. His mother always wrote a note telling the teacher that he had a cough, but we kids all knew that Bobby Decker didn't have a cough—he didn't have a coat. I fingered the ten-dollar bill with growing excitement. I would buy Bobby Decker a coat!

I settled on a red corduroy one that had a hood to it. It looked real warm, and I thought he would like the color. "Is this a Christmas present for someone?" the lady behind the counter asked kindly as I laid my ten dollars down. "Yes," I replied shyly. "It's .... for Bobby." The nice lady smiled at me. I didn't get any change, but she put the coat in a bag and wished me a Merry Christmas.

That evening, Grandma helped me wrap the coat in Christmas paper and ribbon (a little tag fell out of the coat and Grandma tucked it in her Bible). We made a tag and Grandma helped me write, "To Bobby, From Santa Claus" on it—Grandma said that Santa always insisted on secrecy. Then she drove me over to Bobby Decker's house, explaining as we went that I was now and forever officially one of Santa's helpers.

Grandma parked down the street from Bobby's house, and she and I crept as quietly as we could and hid in the bushes by his front walk. Then Grandma gave me a nudge. "All right, Santa Claus," she whispered, "get going."

I took a deep breath, dashed for his front door, threw the present down on his step, punched his doorbell, and flew back to the safety of the bushes and Grandma. Together we waited breathlessly in the darkness for the front door to open. Finally it did, and there stood Bobby.

That night, I realized that those awful rumors about Santa Claus were just what Grandma said they were: ridiculous. Santa was alive and well, and we were on his team.

After Christmas break, Bobby Decker wore his new red coat to school, and went outside to play with the rest of us at recess.

Fifty years haven't dimmed the thrill of those moments spent shivering, beside my Grandma, in Bobby Decker's bushes. I still have the Bible, with the tag tucked inside: $19.95.

December 12

"Speculatious" (St. Nicholas) Cookies

AS YOU REFLECT upon God's great gift of His Son this Advent season, you will undoubtedly be inundated by many modern-day Christmas traditions surrounding Santa Claus and the giving and receiving of gifts. You can bake a traditional Advent cookie called the "Speculatious" as a special way to commemorate the life of the original Santa Claus—a devoted follower of Christ named St. Nicholas.

These delicious rolled cookies can be shaped like stockings or like St. Nick himself. Recipes for the cookie can be found on the internet as well as in many holiday cookbooks. Baking "Speculatious" cookies together as you share the story of St. Nicholas with your children is a fun way to engage them in contemplating the true meaning of the season.

Heavenly Father,

This Christmas season may we understand and emulate the spirit of the true St. Nicholas. May we turn our hearts toward helping the poor and needy. Help us to walk in the humility that he walked in, which helped him to see a need, any need, and do whatever it took to meet it.

Thank You that we can offer comfort, physical, emotional, and spiritual, to those who are suffering, whether from sickness, disease, or depression. May we be especially sensitive this holiday season to those who suffer loneliness and sadness. Let us be a friend to the friendless, a family to the famililess, a comfort to the comfortless, and a hope for the hopeless.

God of all comfort, thank You that because You have comforted us in all our trials and tribulations, we can share Your comfort with others who are facing troubles. We can comfort them with the same comfort You've given us. (2 CORINTHIANS 1:3-4.) *May our home and our hearts be a place of comfort and peace for those who are lonely and hurting this holiday season.*

We praise You, Lord. In Jesus' name,

Amen

From St. Nicholas
to Santa Claus

ST. NICHOLAS IS an Advent saint because his feast day, December 6th, always falls in early Advent. But Nicholas can be considered a good Advent saint for more important reasons as well. There are many stories and legends about him, but what really makes him special is that he was a faithful follower of Jesus Christ. He lived out, every day, the true Christmas spirit we should all carry in our hearts throughout the year—to show God's love to others, especially those in need.

St. Nicholas was born during the third century, sometime around 280 AD in Patara, a village in what is now Turkey. His parents raised him to be a devout Christian. It is said that Nicholas was a miraculous answer to his previously childless parents' prayers. One legend says that when Nicholas was given his first bath, he stood up in the tub and raised his arms as if in prayer. It is also said that little Nicholas refused his mother's milk on Wednesday and Friday evenings, which were times of fasting for the early Christians.

When Nicholas was still young, his parents died in an epidemic. They had been very wealthy, so Nicholas inherited a very wealthy estate. Obeying Jesus' words to "sell what you own and give the money to the poor," Nicholas gave away all his inheritance to travel the countryside helping the needy, the sick, and the suffering. He dedicated his life to serving God.

When still a youth, Nicholas learned of three young sisters in his city whose father, having declined from wealth into direst poverty, could not afford to provide them with dowries. Lest the girls be forced into prostitution or slavery, Nicholas, under cover of darkness, left their father enough gold to enable them all to marry comfortably. According to one version of the story, Nicholas dropped three gold coins in at a window. The coins happened to fall into a stocking belonging to one of the girls, thence originating our custom of hanging up a stocking on Christmas Eve.

Another version of the story says that one went down the chimney and landed in a pair of shoes that had been left on the hearth. Another went into a window and into a pair of stockings left hanging by the fire to dry. In the United States and England, children hang stockings on their bedpost or near a fireplace on Christmas Eve, hoping that it will be filled with treats while they sleep. In Scandinavia, similarminded children leave their shoes on the hearth.

After Nicholas' parents died, his uncle encouraged him to journey to the Holy Land. There as he walked where Jesus walked, he sought to more deeply experience Jesus' life, passion, and resurrection. He returned home by grain ship, and during the voyage a great storm arose threatening the lives of everyone on board. Nicholas prayed calmly but fervently, the storm abated, and everyone was saved. For this act, Nicholas earned the gratitude not only of the sailors but also of the people of the town to which the ship was bound, who narrowly escaped starvation when the grain aboard the ship was saved. St. Nicholas' efforts were not forgotten, and he eventually became the patron saint of sailors, farmers, and bakers.

When he returned from the Holy Land, Nicholas chose to dwell in the city of Myra, only a few miles from his birthplace. After he had lived there for some time in piety and humility, the bishop of that great city died. Now, the elders of the church, uncertain whom to choose as the new bishop, decided to leave the matter in the hands of God. That night the eldest had a dream in which he was told to appoint as the new bishop the first man to enter the church the following morning. Nicholas was accustomed to rise early for prayer, and when he appeared at church that morning at his usual time, he was astonished to find himself appointed the new bishop of Myra—the youngest bishop the church had ever had.

The story of how St. Nicholas became the patron saint of children is a gruesome and fantastic one. Once on his travels, Nicholas stopped to pass the night in the care of an innkeeper. Since the land was undergoing severe famine, the cruel and inhuman innkeeper, at a loss how to provide for his guests, went to the length of murdering three young brothers, who were on their way to study in Athens, intending to serve them to his lodgers as food. Nicholas dreamed of the crime that night, got up, searched the inn, and discovered the remains of the slaughtered boys in a large picking tub. Nicholas prayed over the boys and miraculously, they rose up whole and restored to life.

In France the story is told of three small children, wandering in their play until lost, lured, and captured by an evil butcher. St. Nicholas appears and appeals to God to return them to life and to their families. And so St. Nicholas is the patron and protector of children.

The Roman Emperor Diocletian ruthlessly persecuted Christians and Bishop Nicholas suffered for his faith. He was exiled and imprisoned. The prisons were so full of bishops, priests, and deacons; there was no room for the real criminals. Nicholas was eventually released and died many years later on December 6, AD 343 in Myra. He was buried in his cathedral church, where a unique substance formed in his grave. This liquid substance was said to have healing powers. The anniversary of his death became a day of celebration.

One of the oldest stories showing St. Nicholas as a protector of children takes place long after his death. The townspeople of Myra were celebrating the good saint on the eve of his feast day when a band of Arab pirates from Crete came into the district. They stole treasures from the Church of Saint Nicholas to take away as booty. As they were leaving town, they snatched a young boy, Basilios, to make into a slave. The emir, or ruler, selected Basilios to be his personal cupbearer. So, for the next year Basilios waited on the king, bringing his wine in a beautiful golden cup. As the next St. Nicholas' feast day approached, Basilios' mother would not join in the festivity, as it was now a day of tragedy. However, she was persuaded to have a simple observance at home—with quiet prayers for Basilios' safekeeping. Meanwhile, as Basilios was fulfilling his tasks serving the emir, he was suddenly whisked up and away. St. Nicholas appeared to the terrified boy, blessed him, and set him down at his home back in Myra.

St, Nicholas became the patron saint of Russia when Duke Vladimir, having visited Constantinople in the year 987, returned with a wife, Princess Anna, adopted her religion as that of the Russian people, and brought back to Russia wonderful tales of the saint and a portrait of him. Already by this time, St. Nicholas was being depicted as a majestic old man. In the middle ages, St. Nicholas was often portrayed as a giver of gifts, anticipating an important social function of our modern Santa Claus. By the Renaissance he was often portrayed as a gray-bearded, benevolent-looking old man. In the thirteenth century, the English represented him as riding a goat and bearing gifts of bread and wine.

In Germany, as elsewhere, Christian traditions regarding the saint were mingled with pagan folklore. An old woodcut from this region depicted him as an itinerant eccentric who traveled on a donkey, carried a whip, and hid strange gifts in his hat. The whip was a reminder that at certain times, St. Nicholas was assigned the role of chastiser of naughty children, as well as that of bestower of gifts upon good ones.

During the Protestant Reformation in Germany, the important part that had been played by the saint in Christmas season festivities was severely criticized, and the bearer of gifts at Christmas became the Christ child. But the German word, "Christkindl," was transliterated in English and became "Kriss Kringle." In later years the name Kriss Kringle became associated with Santa Claus.

Some of the most important traits of the Santa Claus we know, including his name, derive from the figure imported by the Dutch to America in the eighteenth century. In December 1773, and again in 1774, a New York newspaper reported that groups of Dutch families had gathered to honor the anniversary of his death. The name Santa Claus evolved from Nick's Dutch nickname, Sinter Klaas, a shortened form of Sint Nikolaas (Dutch for Saint Nicholas). One figure associated with Sinterklass in the seventeenth century, often depicted with switches for naughty children, has long since disappeared in America (though he survives in Holland), as have the saint's white horse and episcopal accoutrements. Also based on Dutch tradition is Santa's mode of entering a house through a snow-covered chimney. The full white beard and the sacks overflowing with gifts for children, however, have remained as attributes of the Santa Claus we know today.

December 13

The Christmas Crèche

AS YOU CENTER your focus more each day on Christ and His coming, involve your whole family in making a homemade nativity scene, called a crèche.

This creative family activity is a wonderful way to reinforce the significance of the Christmas story and the special role of each of the characters involved. The figures of the nativity can be made from paper, yarn, clay, or natural objects like pebbles and twigs. Your family will enjoy saving and adding to your homemade crèche from year to year. Be creative and enjoy this unique way to commemorate the story of Christ's birth.

Heavenly Father,

During this busy Christmas season may we continue to seek after You like the wise men from the East. Like Artaban, may we never give up on our quest to see Your face and know You more, but may we also learn to see Your face in the suffering, lonely, and poor You bring across our path. Lead us daily across the path of someone You want us to touch, to love, to show Jesus to. And not just during the Christmas season, but all year long.

We want to hear You say, "When I was hungry, you gave Me something to eat, and when I was thirsty, you gave Me something to drink. When I was a stranger, you welcomed Me, and when I was naked, you gave Me clothes to wear. When I was sick, you took care of Me, and when I was in jail, you visited Me" (MATTHEW 25:35-36 CEV).

Lord, we lay our gifts at Your feet. They may not be riches, like gold, frankincense, and myrrh, but the gifts we bring are the gifts that came from You, for everything we have, every good and perfect gift comes from You. (JAMES 1:17.) *Nothing we have is our own.*

As we give and receive gifts this Christmas season may the Holy Spirit remind us to be thankful and mindful that You are the source of all good things. May we be willing to give that which You've given us so generously to anyone You may ask us to.

In Jesus' name,

Amen

Artaban's Quest

Adapted from "The Other Wise Man" by Henry Van Dyke

IN THE DAYS when Augustus Caesar was master of many kings and Herod reigned in Jerusalem, there lived in the mountains of Persia, a certain man named Artaban—a Magi. Caspar, Melchoir, and Balthazar were his friends. They had seen the sign of the coming Messiah in the stars and planned to go and worship Him at the appointed time. The three went on to the temple in Babylonia to watch for the new star to appear, while Artaban watched from his home in Ecbatana and shared their news with the other Magi.

But one by one the other men made excuses not to join Artaban and the others in their quest. One even called them foolish to believe that a King would rise from the broken race of Israel.

Before sunrise the following day, Artaban had mounted his swiftest horse, Vasda, and made haste to reach his friends by the designated time. Artaban carried in his tunic, close to his heart, his own tribute to the King—a sapphire, a ruby, and a pearl. When

Artaban and Vasda arrive in the city and begin to make their way to the temple, they pass through a darkly shadowed palm grove.

As she passed into the shadow of the palms Vasda slackened her pace, and began to pick her way more carefully. Near the far end of the darkness she scented some danger or difficulty. It was not in her heart to fly from it—only to be prepared for it, and to meet it wisely, as a good horse should do. At last she gave a quick breath of anxiety and dismay and stood stock-still before a dark object in the shadow of the last palm tree. Artaban dismounted. The dim starlight revealed the form of a man lying across the road. His humble dress and the outline of his haggard face showed that he was probably one of the Hebrews who still dwelt in great numbers around the city. His pale skin bore the mark of the deadly fever which ravaged the marsh-lands in autumn. The chill of death was in his lean hand, and as Artaban released it the arm fell lifelessly back upon the motionless chest.

Artaban turned away with a thought of pity. But as he turned a faint sigh came from the man's lips. The bony fingers gripped the hem of the Magian's robe and held him fast. Artaban's heart leaped to his throat. How could he stay here in the darkness to minister to a dying stranger? If he lingered but for an hour he could hardly reach his friends in time. They would think he had given up the journey and go without him. But if he went on now, the man would surely die. Should he risk the great reward of his faith for the sake of a single deed of charity? Should he turn aside, if only for a moment, from the following of the star, to give a cup of cold water to a poor, perishing Hebrew? "God of truth and purity," he prayed, "direct me in the holy path, the way of wisdom which You only know."

Artaban turned back to the sick man. He brought water from one of the small canals nearby, and moistened the sufferer's brow and mouth. He mixed a draught of one of those simple but potent remedies which he always carried with him—for the Magians were physicians as well as astrologers—and poured it slowly between the colorless lips. Hour after hour he labored as only a skillful healer of disease can do. At last the man's strength returned; he sat up and looked around.

"Who are you?" he said, in the rude dialect of the country, "and why have you come here to bring back my life?"

"I am Artaban the Magian, and I am going to Jerusalem in search of One who is to be born King of the Jews. I dare not delay any longer. But here is all I have left of bread and wine, and here is a potion of healing herbs. When your strength is restored you can find the dwellings of the Hebrews among the houses of Babylon." The Jew raised his trembling hand solemnly to heaven. "May the God of Abraham and Isaac and Jacob bless and prosper the journey of the merciful, and bring him in peace to his desired haven. I have nothing to give you in return—only this: I can tell you where the Messiah must be sought. Our prophets have said that He should be born not in Jerusalem, but in Bethlehem of Judah."

It was already long past midnight. Artaban rode in haste, but when he arrived at the Temple of the Seven Spheres, he could discern no trace of his friends. He dismounted and climbed to the highest terrace, looking out toward the west. The huge desolation of the marshes stretched away to the horizon. There was no sign of the caravan of the Wise Men, far or near. At the edge of the terrace he saw a little pile of broken bricks and under them a note.

"We have waited past midnight, and can delay no longer. We go to find the King. Follow us across the desert."

Artaban sat down upon the ground and covered his head in despair. "How can I cross the desert," said he, "with no food and with a spent horse? I must return to Babylon, sell my sapphire, and buy a train of camels and provision for the journey. I may never overtake my friends. Only God the merciful knows whether I shall lose the sight of the King because I tarried to show mercy."

Artaban journeyed on through the desolate wasteland, moving steadily onward, until he drew near to Bethlehem, weary, but full of hope, bearing his ruby and his pearl to offer to the King. "For now at last," he said, "I shall surely find Him, though I be alone, and later than my brethren." The streets of the village seemed to be deserted, and Artaban wondered whether the men had all gone up to the hill pastures to bring down their sheep.

From the open door of a cottage Artaban heard the sound of a woman singing softly. He entered and found a young mother hushing her baby to rest. She told him of the strangers from the Far East who had appeared in the village three days ago, and how they said that a star had led them to the place where Joseph of Nazareth was lodging with his wife and newborn child, and how they had paid reverence to the child and given Him many rich gifts. "But the travelers disappeared again," she continued, "as suddenly as they had come. The man of Nazareth took the child and His mother, and fled away that same night secretly, and it was whispered that they were going to Egypt. Ever since, there has been a spell upon the village; something evil hangs over it. They say that the Roman soldiers are coming from Jerusalem to force a new tax from us, and the men have driven the flocks and herds far back among the hills and hidden themselves to escape it."

The young mother laid the baby in its cradle, and rose to minister to the wants of her strange guest. She set food before him, the plain fare of peasants, but willingly offered, and therefore full of refreshment for the soul as well as for the body. Artaban accepted it gratefully and as he ate, the child fell into a happy slumber, and murmured sweetly in its dreams. But suddenly there came the noise of a wild confusion in the streets, a shrieking and wailing of women's voices: "The soldiers! The soldiers of Herod! They are killing our children."

The young mother's face grew white with terror. She clasped her child to her bosom and crouched motionless in the darkest corner of the room. Artaban went quickly and stood in the doorway of the house. The soldiers came hurrying down the street with bloody hands and dripping swords. At the sight of the imposing stranger they hesitated. The captain of the band approached the threshold to thrust him aside, but Artaban did not move. He said in a low voice, "I am all alone in this place, and I am waiting to give this jewel to the prudent captain who will leave me in peace." He showed the ruby, glistening in the hollow of his hand like a great drop of blood. The captain was amazed at the splendor of the gem, and the hard lines of greed wrinkled around his lips. He stretched out his hand and took the ruby. "March on!" he cried to his men. "There is no child here. The house is empty."

Artaban reentered the cottage. He turned his face to the east and prayed: "God of truth, forgive my sin! I have lied to save the life of a child. And now two of my gifts are gone. I have spent for man that which was meant for God. Shall I ever be worthy to see the face of the King?" But the woman, weeping for joy in the shadow behind him, said gently, "Because you have saved the life of my little one, may the Lord bless you and keep you; the Lord make His face to shine upon you and be gracious to you; the Lord lift up His countenance upon you and give you peace."

Afterward, Artaban continued on to Egypt, seeking everywhere for traces of the household that had come down from Bethlehem. Years passed, and Artaban wondered if Tigranes was right. Was he on a search that could never succeed?

His search eventually led him to an obscure house where there lived a Hebrew rabbi. The old man, bending over the rolls of parchment on which the prophecies of Israel were written, read aloud the words which foretold the sufferings of the promised Messiah.

"And remember, my son," said he, fixing his eyes upon the face of Artaban, "what you seek is not to be found in a palace, nor among the rich and powerful. The light for which the world is waiting is a new light, the glory that will rise out of patient and triumphant suffering. The kingdom which is to be established forever is a new kingdom, the royalty of unconquerable love. I do not know how this will come to pass. But this I do know: Those who seek Him will do well to look among the poor and the oppressed."

Artaban left the man and continued to travel from place to place. He passed through countries where famine lay heavy upon the land, and the poor were crying for bread. He made his dwelling in plague-stricken cities where the sick were languishing in helpless misery. He visited the oppressed and the afflicted. In all this world of anguish though he found none to worship, he found many to help. He fed the hungry, clothed the naked, healed the sick, and comforted the captive. His years passed swiftly and it almost seemed as if he had forgotten his quest.

Three-and-thirty years of the life of Artaban had passed away, and he was still a pilgrim and a seeker after light. His hair, once black as night, was now white as the wintry snow. His eyes that once flashed like flames of fire were dull as embers smoldering among the ashes. Worn and weary and ready to die, but still looking for the King, he had come to Jerusalem one last time. He had often visited the holy city before, without finding any trace of the family who had fled from Bethlehem long ago. But now it seemed as if he must make one more effort, and something whispered in his heart that at last he might succeed. It was the season of the Passover. The city was thronged with strangers. The children of Israel, scattered in far lands, had returned to the Temple for the great feast. But on this day the crowd was agitated and restless.

The sky was veiled with a portentous gloom. Artaban joined a group of people from his own country, Parthian Jews who had come up to keep the Passover, and asked of them the cause of the tumult, and where they were going. "We are going," they answered, "to the place called Golgotha, outside the city walls, where there is to be an execution. Have you not heard what has happened? Two famous robbers are to be crucified, and with them another, called Jesus of Nazareth, a man who has done many wonderful works among the people, so that they love Him greatly. But the priests and elders have said that He must die, because He said He was the Son of God. And Pilate has sent Him to the cross because He said that He was the King of the Jews."

How strangely these familiar words fell upon Artaban's tired heart! They had led him for a lifetime over land and sea. And now they came to him like a message of despair. The King had arisen, but he had been denied and cast out. He was about to perish. Could it be the same King who had been born in Bethlehem thirty-three years ago, at whose birth the star had appeared, and of whose coming the prophets had spoken? Artaban's heart beat unsteadily. But he said within himself: *The ways of God are stranger than the thoughts of men, and it may be that I shall find the King, at last, in the hands of His enemies, and shall come in time to offer my pearl for His ransom.*

So the old man followed the multitude toward the Damascus gate. Just beyond the entrance of the guardhouse a troop of Macedonian soldiers came down the street, dragging a young girl. As the Magian paused to look at her with compassion, she broke suddenly from the hands of her tormentors, and threw herself at his feet, clasping him around the knees. She had seen his white cap and the winged circle on his breast. "Have pity on me," she cried, "and save me, for the sake of the God of Purity! I am a daughter of the true religion which is taught by the Magi. My father was a merchant of Parthia, but he is dead, and I am seized for his debts to be sold as a slave. Save me!" Artaban trembled. It was the old conflict in his soul, which had come to him in the palm grove of Babylon and in the cottage at Bethlehem—the conflict between the expectation of faith and the impulse of love. Twice a gift which he had consecrated to the worship of religion had been drawn to the service of humanity. This was the third trial, the final and irrevocable choice. Was it his great opportunity, or his last temptation? He could not tell. Only one thing was sure to his divided heart—to rescue this helpless girl would be a true deed of love. He took the pearl from his bosom. Never had it seemed so luminous, so radiant, and so full of tender, living luster. He laid it in the girl's hand. "This is thy ransom, daughter! It is the last of my treasures which I kept for the King."

While he spoke, the sky grew dark and the earth shuddered. The walls of the houses rocked to and fro. Stones crashed into the street. Dust filled the air. The soldiers fled in terror, reeling like drunken men. But Artaban and the girl crouched helpless beneath the wall of the Pretoria. What had he to fear? What had he to hope? He had given away the last remnant of his tribute for the King. His quest was over. It had failed. But he was at peace. He knew that all was well, because he had done the best he could from day to day.

The ground shivered once more. A heavy tile, shaken from the roof, fell and struck the old man on the temple. He lay breathless and pale, with his gray head resting on the young girl's shoulder, blood trickling from the wound. As she bent over him, fearing that he was dead, there came a still small voice through the twilight, like music sounding from a distance. The girl turned to see if someone had spoken from the window above them, but she saw no one. Then the old man's lips began to move, as if in answer, and she heard him say in the Parthian tongue, "Not so, my Lord! For when did I see you hungry and fed you? Or thirsty, and gave you drink? When did I see you a stranger, and took you in? Or naked, and clothed you? When did I see you sick or in prison, and came unto you? Three-and-thirty years have I looked for you; but I have never seen your face, nor ministered to you, my King." And again the maid heard the sweet voice, very faint and far away. But now it seemed as though she understood the words: "Verily I say unto you. Inasmuch as you have done it unto one of the least of these my brethren, you have done it unto me." A calm radiance of wonder and joy lighted Artaban's pale face like the first ray of dawn on a snowy mountain peak. A long breath of relief exhaled gently from his lips. His journey was ended. His treasures were accepted. The Other Wise Man had found the King.

December 14

Gathering Straws for the Manger

ONE SPECIAL TASK of the Advent season is to prepare your heart for the coming of Jesus—both in celebration of His birth and in expectation of His return. You can symbolically act out this preparation process along with your family by gathering straws for Jesus' manger.

Set aside a bunch of straws to be given to members of your family as rewards for their individual good deeds and acts of service to one another. The straws should be added to the empty manger one at a time in anticipation of the placement of the baby Jesus in the manger on Christmas Eve or Christmas Day. This simple symbolic gesture will help maintain an attitude of eager expectation in your hearts each day of the Advent season.

Father God,

We pray today that everyone around us—friends, family, neighbors, and strangers—will know and experience Your love this holiday season. Using the words of Paul's prayer for the Ephesians, we pray that out of Your glorious riches, You may strengthen them with power through Your Spirit in their inner beings, so that Christ may dwell in their hearts through faith. And we pray that they would be rooted and established in love, and may have power, together with all the saints, to grasp how wide and long and high and deep is the love of Christ, and to know this love that surpasses knowledge—that they may be filled to the measure of all the fullness of God.

Now to You who are able to do immeasurably more than all we ask or imagine, according to Your power that is at work within us, to You be glory in the church and in Christ Jesus throughout all generations, for ever and ever! (EPHESIANS 4:16-21.)

Thank You, Father God, that You are well able to bring these things to pass. You are well able to provide, through us and others, for those in need. May we be willing to give up the things we think we need or want in order to meet the needs that You ask us to.

In Jesus' precious name,

Amen

The Best Christmas Ever

Author Unknown

PA NEVER HAD much compassion for the lazy or those who squandered their means and then never had enough for the necessities. But for those who were genuinely in need, his heart was as big as all outdoors. It was from him that I learned the greatest joy in life comes from giving, not from receiving.

It was Christmas Eve 1881. I was fifteen years old and feeling like the world had caved in on me because there just hadn't been enough money to buy me the rifle that I'd wanted so bad that year for Christmas.

We did the chores early that night for some reason. I just figured Pa wanted a little extra time so we could read the Bible. So after supper was over I took my boots off and stretched out in front of the fireplace and waited for Pa to get down the old Bible. I was still feeling sorry for myself and, to be honest, I wasn't in much of a mood to read the Scriptures. But Pa didn't get out the old Bible; instead he bundled up and went outside. I couldn't figure out what was going on, because we had already done all the chores. I didn't worry about it long though; I was too busy wallowing in self-pity.

Soon Pa came back in. It was a cold, clear night out and there was ice in his beard. "Come on, Matt," he said. "Bundle up good, it's cold out tonight."

I was really upset then. Not only was I not going to get the rifle for Christmas, now Pa was dragging me out in the cold. We'd already done all the chores and I couldn't think of anything else that needed doing, especially not on a night like this. But I knew Pa was not very patient about one dragging one's feet when he's told them to do something, so I got up and put my boots back on and got my cap, coat, and mittens. Ma gave me a mysterious smile as I opened the door to leave the house.

Once outside, I became even more dismayed. Standing in front of the house was the work team, already hitched to the big sled. Whatever it was we were going to do wasn't going to be a quick little job. We never hitched up the big sled unless we were going to haul a big load. Pa was already up on the seat, reins in hand. I reluctantly climbed up beside him. The cold was already biting at me. I wasn't happy.

When I was on the seat, Pa pulled the sled around the house and stopped in front of the woodshed. He got off and I followed. "I think we'll put on the high sideboards," he said. "Here, help me." The high sideboards! It had been a bigger job than I wanted to do with just the low sideboards on, but whatever it was we were going to do would be a lot bigger with the high sideboards on.

When we had exchanged the sideboards Pa went into the woodshed and came out with an armload of wood—the wood I'd spent all summer hauling down from the mountain, and then all fall sawing into blocks and splitting. What was he doing? Finally I said something. "Pa," I asked, "what are you doing?"

"You been by the Widow Jensen's lately?" he asked.

The Widow Jensen lived about two miles down the road. Her husband had died a year or so before and left her with three children, the oldest being eight.

"Yeah," I said. "Why?"

"I rode by just today," Pa said. "Little Jakey was out digging around in the woodpile trying to find a few chips. They're out of wood, Matt." That was all he said and then he turned and went back into the wood-shed for another armload of wood. This time I followed him.

We loaded the sled so high that I began to wonder if the horses would be able to pull it. Finally, Pa said we'd loaded enough, then we went to the smoke house and Pa took down a big ham and a side of bacon. He handed them to me and told me to put them in the sled and wait. When he returned he was carrying a sack of flour over his right shoulder and a smaller sack of something in his left hand. "What's in the little sack?" I asked.

"Shoes. They're out of shoes. Little Jakey just had gunny sacks wrapped around his feet when he was out in the woodpile this morning. I got the children a little candy too. It just wouldn't be Christmas without a little candy." We rode the two miles to Widow Jensen's place pretty much in silence.

We didn't have much by worldly standards. Of course, we did have a big woodpile, though most of what was left now was still in the form of logs that I would have to saw and split before we could use it. We also had meat and flour, so we could spare that, but I knew we didn't have any money, so why was Pa buying shoes and candy to give away? Really, why was he doing any of this? Widow Jensen had closer neighbors than us. It shouldn't have been our concern.

We came in from the blind side of the Jensen house and unloaded the wood as quietly as possible, and then we took the meat and flour and shoes to the door. When we knocked the door opened a crack and a timid voice asked, "Who is it?"

"Lucas Miles, Ma'am, and my son, Matt. Could we come in for a bit?"

Widow Jensen opened the door and let us in. She had a blanket wrapped around her shoulders. The children were wrapped in another and were sitting in front of the fireplace by a very small fire. "We brought you a few things, Ma'am," Pa said and set down the sack of flour. I put the meat on the table.

Then Pa handed her the sack that had the shoes in it. She opened it hesitantly and took the shoes out one pair at a time. There was a pair for her and one for each of the children—sturdy shoes, shoes that would last. I watched her carefully. She bit her lower lip to keep it from trembling and then tears filled her eyes and started running down her cheeks. She looked up at Pa like she wanted to say something, but it wouldn't come out.

"We brought a load of wood too, Ma'am," Pa said, then he turned to me and said, "Matt, go bring enough in to last for awhile. Let's get that fire up to size and heat this place up."

I wasn't the same person when I went back out to bring in the wood. I had a big lump in my throat and, much as I hate to admit it, there were tears in my eyes too. In my mind I kept seeing those three kids huddled around the fireplace and their mother standing there with tears running down her cheeks and so much gratitude in her heart that she couldn't speak. My heart swelled within me and a joy filled my soul that I'd never known before. I had given at Christmas many times before, but never when it had made so much difference.

I soon had the fire blazing and everyone's spirits soared. The kids started giggling when Pa handed them each a piece of candy and Widow Jensen looked on with a smile that probably hadn't crossed her face for a long time. She finally turned to us. "God bless you," she said. "I know the Lord Himself has sent you."

In spite of myself, the lump returned to my throat and tears welled up in my eyes. I was sure that a better man than Pa had never walked the earth. I started remembering all the times he had gone out of his way for Ma and me, and many others. The list seemed endless as I thought on it.

Pa insisted that everyone try on the shoes before we left. I was amazed when they all fit and I wondered how he had known what sizes to get. Then I guessed that if he was on an errand for the Lord that the Lord would make sure he got the right sizes.

Tears were running down Widow Jensen's face again when we stood up to leave. Pa took each of the kids in his big arms and gave them a hug. They clung to him and didn't want us to go. I could see that they missed their pa, and I was glad that I still had mine.

At the door Pa turned to Widow Jensen and said, "The Mrs. wanted me to invite you and the children over for Christmas dinner tomorrow. The turkey will be more than the three of us can eat, and a man can get cantankerous if he has to eat leftover turkey. We'll be by to get you about eleven. It'll be nice to have some little ones around again. Matt here hasn't been little for quite a spell."

Widow Jensen nodded and said, "Thank you, Brother Miles. I don't have to say, 'May the Lord bless you,' I know for certain that He will."

Out on the sled I felt a warmth that came from deep within and I didn't even notice the cold. When we had gone a ways, Pa turned to me and said, "Matt, I want you to know something. Your ma and me have been tucking a little money away here and there all year so we could buy that rifle for you, but we didn't have quite enough. Then yesterday a man who owed me a little money from years back came by to make things square. Your ma and I were real excited, thinking that now we could get you that rifle, and I started into town this morning to do just that. But on the way I saw little Jakey out scratching in the woodpile with his feet wrapped in those gunny sacks and I knew what I had to do. So, son, I spent the money for shoes and a little candy for those children. I hope you understand."

I understood, and my eyes became wet with tears again. I understood very well, and I was so glad Pa had done it. Just then the rifle seemed very low on my list of priorities. Pa had given me a lot more. He had given me the look on Widow Jensen's face and the radiant smiles of her three children. For the rest of my life, whenever I saw any of the Jensens, or split a block of wood, I remembered. And each time I remembered it brought back that same joy I felt riding home beside Pa that night. Pa had given me much more than a rifle that night, he had given me the best Christmas of my life.

December 15

Lighting of the Third Candle
in the Advent Wreath

THE ROSE-COLORED candle is the third candle to be lighted as part of the Advent wreath and is symbolic of our joy at the coming of Christ. Gather your family for a joy-filled celebration as you light the third candle together.

Create a festive atmosphere for the lighting of the candle by sharing a special meal or activity you all enjoy. Then, ask each member of your family to choose a character from the Christmas story (including the shepherds, wise men, Mary, and Joseph) and describe the joy he or she must have felt at Christ's birth. Pray together that God will help your family portray His joy to the world around you, especially in this season of celebrating His birth.

Father God,

We come before You with great joy. We praise You for the joy You have given us in Jesus Christ. The joy we have in Him gives us strength day by day. We pray that the joy in our hearts overflows to those around us and touches their hearts with Your joy and peace.

We pray that "all who take refuge in You will rejoice; let them sing joyful praises forever. Protect them, so all who love Your name may be filled with joy" (PSALM 5:11 NLT). *Thank You, Lord, that You've promised we would go out in joy and be led by Your peace.* (ISAIAH 55:12.)

We also pray for those who need Your joy right now, "May the God of hope fill you with all joy and peace as you trust in him, so that you may overflow with hope by the power of the Holy Spirit" (ROMANS 15:13).

Father, Your Word says that for the joy set before Him, Jesus endured the cross, so that we could become Your children. (HEBREWS 12:2.) *Our redemption was a joy to Him! Thank You, Lord. We rejoice today in Your redeeming love!*

In Jesus' name,

Amen ❧

Amy Angel

Author Unknown

THERE ARE ADVANTAGES and disadvantages to living in a small town. One advantage is that everyone knows everyone else. One disadvantage is that everyone knows everyone else.

Everyone knew Amy Williams, only child. She had been born seventeen years ago, crippled in body if not in spirit. No one had expected her to live, but she had. Everyone knew Amy Williams. Her hunched back and twisted spine were recognizable at a distance. Here she sat outside the choir room door, agonizing.

What am I doing here? she thought to herself. *I'll never be chosen for a part.*

One advantage to living in a small town is that they develop traditions. The annual Christmas pageant was a Marysvale tradition. It had been performed for so many years that no one could remember when it had begun or who had written it, but it had become the focal point of the Christmas season for many of the townspeople.

I don't want to go through the rejection again, thought Amy. *I try not to care, but I do. I don't want to be hurt anymore.*

More people tried out each year for parts in the pageant than could possibly be used. Young children hoped to be shepherd boys, older ones the shepherds or the wise men. Those who sang hoped to be part of the angelic choir. A chosen few hoped to play the innkeeper, the angel of the Lord, Joseph, Mary. Many were turned away, for the stage in the old schoolhouse was small. The choir was only a dozen or so voices.

Mr. Simons will never choose me for a part. I just don't fit. But at least I don't have to audition in front of Mrs. Prendergast, mused Amy.

Mrs. Prendergast had been the music teacher at Marysvale High School for more than thirty years. She had cast, directed, and accompanied the pageant for many years. When Amy was a freshman, three years ago, she had tried out for the pageant. Mrs. Prendergast had taken one look at Amy's misshapen body and said, "Child, you just don't fit. I don't remember anywhere in the script where it calls for a crippled girl." Without singing a single note, Amy had been thrust back through the choral room door. She shuffled home hurt and humiliated and vowed never to try out again. Then . . . Mrs. Prendergast retired.

This year they had a new choral teacher, Mr. Simons. He was the opposite of Mrs. Prendergast. He led with love and compassion. Amy liked him from the first. He demanded perfection, but understood when it was not reached. He coached and corrected with kindness. And he sang himself with such power.

One day he asked Amy to see him after class. He suggested she audition for the pageant.

I ought to leave now and avoid the pain. There's no place for a girl like me in the pageant. I don't want to be rejected again. Still . . . Mr. Simons asked me to try out. I owe it to him. But he'll never choose me. I'm going to leave before it's my turn. As Amy struggled to her feet, the door was pushed open and Mr. Simons called out, "Amy, you're next."

When she finished singing, Mr. Simons said, "Thank you, Amy. The list will be posted tomorrow."

She struggled all night. Her mind went back and forth between the reality of knowing she didn't fit and the great need to be accepted. By morning she had a knot in the pit of her stomach and could not bring herself to look at the list on the choir room door. But as her third-period music class approached, she knew that avoiding it would not change the outcome.

Timidly, fearfully, she looked at the list. The heavenly choir was listed at the bottom of the page. As she suspected, her name wasn't there. *Rejected again!* She turned to enter the class when out of the corner of her eye she saw her name listed at the top of the page. She, Amy Williams, had been chosen to sing the only solo part in the whole pageant. She was to be the angel of the Lord. She was to sing to the Christ child, the Son of God.

There had to be a mistake. Certainly Mr. Simons would not put her in that part. It was so visible. "Amy," called Mr. Simons from the piano, "we need to talk about your part after class."

Class seemed to last forever. Finally it ended and she made her way to Mr. Simon's side. "You wanted to talk to me?"

"Amy, I hope this doesn't upset you, but I need to stage your part a little differently this year." *Hidden offstage*, she thought. Mr. Simons continued: "I would like to have a pyramid built, place the other angels on it, and put you at the very top. I know in the past they've put the angel just a bit above the shepherds, but I think the message you sing is the central part of the pageant." The years of hurt exploded. "You don't want me in the middle of the stage! Won't the way I look ruin the whole thing? You don't want me where everybody will stare at me!"

"Amy, I chose you because you deserve the part. What you think of yourself, I cannot change. I have no problem with you singing this part, and in this pageant the angel of the Lord is center stage. You must come to peace with yourself or you must tell me to choose someone else for the part. It is your decision."

That night Amy made her decision. The rehearsals were exhausting. Her body ached after struggling to the top of the pyramid, but great joy filled her heart. One advantage to living in a small town is that when there is a community event, everyone attends. And so it was the Sunday before Christmas when the whole town of Marysvale attended the Christmas pageant.

Amy Williams, only child, broken in body but not in spirit, stood on the top of a silver-white pyramid and sang her heart out to the Christ child.

"What Child is this, who, laid to rest, On Mary's lap is sleeping? . . ."

Never had the angel sung more sweetly. No one had realized how sick Amy really was because they were so used to seeing her broken body. So it was a shock when she died that next Tuesday. Her mother conveyed a last request from Amy to Mr. Simons. Would he please sing at her funeral?

And so that Christmas Eve two of Amy's classmates, helped Mr. Simons from his wheelchair and supported him as he sang for a daughter of God, as she had sung for His Son. There are advantages to living in a small town.

December 16

The Box of Good Deeds

ADVENT IS A wonderful time to reflect upon the blessings God has given you and the calling of Christ to reach out to those around you. You can create a "box of good deeds" as a tangible daily reminder of this special responsibility during the remainder of the Advent season.

Construct you own "box of good deeds" by decorating an empty shoe box or purchasing a seasonal tin. Then fill your box with slips of paper detailing good deeds you'd like to do such as visiting a shut-in neighbor or delivering a batch of cookies to a local nursing home. Draw a new "good deed" from the box every day or every few days as you have time. Your acts of service will help center you and your family on the true significance of the Advent season.

Lord,

Today we pray that we would be a comfort to the lonely and hurting people around us, especially those who have lost loved ones. We pray that they would feel Your love in us and realize that they are part of a family—Your family.

As we seek to do good deeds and keep our focus on others, rather than getting caught up in selfishness, keep our eyes open to all the opportunities around us. Help us to see even the things that we might think are very small things that are easy to do, so easy that we sometimes forget what an impact a simple smile can have.

Remind us to keep the spirit of doing good deeds in our home, with our immediate family, whom we can sometimes take for granted. Let us see our family members through Your eyes. Show us things we can do, large or small, that would truly be a blessing to them.

May we provoke one another on to love and good works. (HEBREWS 10:24.)

In Jesus' name,

Amen

A Gift from the Children:
A Christmas Miracle

Author Unknown

HELEN. DEAR, SWEET, elderly, Helen—such a beloved lady and friend to all who knew her. She wasn't a young spry chicken anymore. She was well into her 90's, and not quite as energetic and bubbly as when she first visited the church so many years before. The year 1998 was not to be a very kind year to Helen. She had suffered many losses. She had lost her beloved husband six years before, but this year she seemed to have lost it all.

After her husband passed away, she had moved in with her daughter, Becky, and her young grand-daughter, Jennifer. They saved her from the loneliness she would surely have endured without their love. They grew closer every day, and each new day, life brought them more to be grateful for. They knew they were blessed and they always remembered their blessings in prayer.

Jennifer was only two years old when Helen first came to live with them. She was cute as a button, rambunctious, outgoing, and always joyful and singing. Becky and Helen used to joke how it took the two of them to even half keep up with the whirlwind they nicknamed "Sunshine."

Jennifer was curious as a cat, and filled the day with endless questions—some deep, some comical, and each one demanding answers! Her mother and her grandma were diligent to never carelessly brush her questions aside. They answered each and every one to the best of their ability.

Jennifer grew into a brilliant young lady, and everyone predicted a bright and sunny future for the special little girl. But sometimes those things we're sure of don't come to pass.

One night, driving home from the store, Becky and Jennifer were hit head-on by a drunk driver. It was a mistake—a horrid mistake. If it weren't for a flat tire, they would have been home long before the intoxicated man drove down their street. Nobody can predict the future. That night Becky and Jennifer's bright future was scattered among the broken glass and the shredded steel. They were gone. Once again, Helen was alone.

The sorrow that lived in Helen's heart surely should have killed her, she thought. The agony of losing those closest to her, the loneliness of being all alone in a house as quiet as a tomb, and the emptiness of having nothing more to live for were more than she could bear. She continued to pray and go to church faithfully every Sunday. She was always polite to the concerned parishioners around her, but she was so sad. She had changed—withered, deflated, crumbled. She seemed hardly able to put one foot in front of the other. Her joyous laughter was seldom heard, her excitement and zest for life were simply gone. She seemed to just be waiting for her turn to go be with her loved ones.

Naturally, all the other parishioners saw the change. They felt her sadness and loneliness. She had always been such a pillar of strength, a friend in need, someone who could be counted on when the rest of the world had checked out. She was always there, in every way, for everyone. But now, she wasn't there at all, and nobody seemed to know how to comfort her or help her.

Months passed. It was now December, and the holiday season was proving to be harder than Helen had imagined it would be—and even lonelier. She still went through the motions of living, kept up appearances, prayed, and was kind to everyone she met. Yet she felt like she was slowing dying inside. She often wondered if she would see Christmas this year.

Then, the second Sunday of December, the Sunday school teacher came to her with a special request. Would she be kind enough to help with trimming the tree that stood in the middle of the children's classroom? Each child had handmade a special ornament to place on the tree, and they needed assistance and adult supervision. Helen tried to gracefully decline, but the teacher smiled, and said that the children had specifically requested that she be the assistant this year. It was important to them for some reason, the teacher said.

The night of the special event, Helen was dressed as immaculately as always, and wore the best smile she could muster. The sight of the young children was bittersweet. Their laughter and playfulness were refreshing, but they also held memories of Jennifer. It had only been four short months and she felt the pain as acutely now as the day it happened.

For the first time in months though, you could occasionally see the light return to her eyes. She decided she was happy that the children had thought to invite her, and thankful that she had decided to come join in the merriment. She felt more alive than she had since that dreadful day.

Most of the ornaments had already been placed on the tree when an excited, almost giddy, group of children came to her and took her by the hand. They led her to an ornate, red velvet chair that the teacher had pushed into the center of the room, and they begged for her to sit down. Curious, and a little apprehensive, Helen good-heartedly obeyed. You could see a tiny smile light up the corner of her mouth as she wondered what they were up to.

A group of five girls and four boys sat in front of her splendid chair, smiling up at her with eyes moist with tears of happiness, trying very hard not to give away their secret. In the middle of the group sat a magnificent gold, gift-wrapped box addressed to: "Our Grandma, with Love."

Eight-year-old Christine stood before Helen, tears overflowing, smiling from ear to ear. Christine had always been special to Helen, for she had been Jennifer's best friend since they were both toddlers. Helen and Christine had spent much time together over the years, and they had grown close as well. She placed the box in Helen's lap and the whole group rose in unison, and began to sing for an amazed and delighted Helen, who seemed to be crying and laughing and praying all at the same time!

With pride in their eyes, and love in their voices, and their notes sometimes off-key, they told Helen the reason that she was there. It was easy to see that the children had written the words of the song just for her—a gift to be cherished, wonderful memories to last forevermore. Each of the nine small children had already lost their grandmother or had never even known her. This was a very special celebration and union—the beginning of a special new family bonding, growing, and loving—and sharing a very special Christmas.

One by one, the children unpacked the special ornaments they had made, and proudly showed Helen their surprise for her. Each ornament was addressed, "To my special Grandma, with Love—on our First Christmas." Every ornament was unique, special, splendid, and every one was a miracle beyond belief, to a heart so desperately in pain.

Once again, proving that sometimes life surprises us, Christmas 1998 wasn't unkind to Helen whatsoever. No, this Christmas was a new beginning, a brand-new start, and nine new reasons to celebrate many more Christmases to come.

Over the next two weeks Helen became a human dynamo! She baked, she decorated, she sang, and she filled her house with so much Christmas cheer until at last it was filled with warmth again. She invited her nine special grandkids over and celebrated Christmas as only a very special, wonderful grandma knows how to do—filled to the brim with magical memories that only the nine most special grandchildren on earth could ever have provided.

December 17

The Christ Child's Birthday Cake

AS YOU ENDEAVOR to stay in the mind-set of joy and anticipation this Advent season, baking a cake to commemorate Christ's birth is one tangible (and yummy!) way to express your celebration.

The symbolism of the birthday cake is especially meaningful for small children, who are familiar with waiting in anxious anticipation for their own birthdays. Make your special cake using a favorite recipe or purchase a store-bought birthday cake that can be shared with your whole family. Then, enjoy this lovely and lighthearted reminder of Christ's birth together.

Heavenly Father,

We know that children are special to You. Jesus said, "Let the children come to me, and don't try to stop them! People who are like these children belong to God's kingdom" (MATTHEW 19:14 CEV).

And we know that while we sit here in our comfortable, warm home, children all around the world are suffering—homelessness, hunger, nakedness, sickness, disease, abuse, neglect, and the list goes on. We know that we can't possibly touch every single one of those children, but You can. You can use us, and others around the world who hear Your voice, to touch the suffering children of the world in some small, or big, way.

Thank You for the opportunity to make a child's life better. Give us wisdom on the right organizations and charities to give to, but also give us the chance to directly affect a child.

May we be Your arms and hands to any child who needs Your love today.

In Jesus' name,

Amen

The Christmas Cuckoo

By Frances Browne

ONCE UPON A time there stood in the midst of a bleak moor, in the North Country, a certain village. All its inhabitants were poor, for their fields were barren, and they had little trade; but the poorest of them all were two brothers called Scrub and Spare, who followed the cobbler's craft. Their hut was built of clay and wattles (rods and twigs) and the roof did not entirely keep out the rain, but they worked there in most brotherly friendship, though with little encouragement.

Then one unlucky day a new cobbler arrived in the village. He had lived in the capital city of the kingdom and, by his own account, cobbled for the queen and the princesses. He set up his stall in a neat cottage with two windows. The villagers soon found that one patch of his would outwear two of the brothers'. In short, all the mending left Scrub and Spare, and went to the new cobbler.

The brothers were poor that winter and their barley and cabbages had not produced much that season. When Christmas came they had nothing to feast on but a barley loaf and a piece of rusty bacon. Worse than that, the snow was very deep and they could get no firewood.

Their hut stood at the end of the village and beyond it spread the bleak moor, now all white and silent. But that moor had once been a forest. Great roots of old trees were still to be found in it, loosened from the soil and laid bare by the winds and rains. One of these, a rough, gnarled log, lay by their door, half of it above the snow, and Spare said to his brother, "Shall we sit here cold on Christmas while the great root lies yonder? Let us chop it up for firewood. The work will make us warm."

"No," said Scrub, "it's not right to chop wood on Christmas. Besides, that root is too hard to be broken with any hatchet."

"Hard or not, we must have a fire," replied Spare. "Come, brother, help me. Poor as we are there is nobody in the village who will have such a Yule log as ours." Scrub liked a little grandeur and in hopes of having a fine Yule log, both brothers strained and strove with all their might till the great old root was safe on the hearth, and beginning to crackle and blaze with the red embers.

In high glee the cobblers sat down to their bread and bacon. The door was shut, for there was nothing but cold moonlight and snow outside; but the hut, strewn with fir boughs and ornamented with holly, looked cheerful as the ruddy blaze flared up and rejoiced their hearts.

Then suddenly from out of the blazing root they heard: "Cuckoo! Cuckoo!" as plain as ever the spring bird's voice came over the moor on a May morning.

"What is that?" said Scrub, terribly frightened.

And out of the deep hole at the side of the root, which the fire had not reached, flew a large, gray cuckoo, and lit on the table before them. Much as the cobblers had been surprised, they were still more so when it said, "Good gentlemen, what season is this?"

"It's Christmas," said Spare.

"Then a merry Christmas to you!" said the cuckoo. "I went to sleep in the hollow of that old root one evening last summer, and never woke till the heat of your fire made me think it was summer again. But now since you have burned my lodging, let me stay in your hut till the spring comes round. I only want a hole to sleep in, and when I go on my travels next summer be assured I will bring you some presents for your trouble."

"Welcome," said Spare. "I'll make you a good warm hole in the thatch, but you must be hungry after that long sleep. Here is a slice of barley bread. Come, help us to keep Christmas!"

The cuckoo ate up the slice, drank water from a brown jug, and flew into the snug hole which Spare scooped for it in the thatch of the hut.

Scrub said he was afraid it wouldn't be lucky, but as it slept on and the days passed he forgot his fears.

So the snow melted, the heavy rains came, the cold grew less, the days lengthened, and one sunny morning the brothers were awakened by the cuckoo shouting its cry to let them know spring had come.

"Now I'm going on my travels," said the bird, "over the world to tell men of the spring. Give me another slice of barley bread to help me on my journey, and tell me what presents I shall bring you at the twelve month's end."

Scrub would have been angry with his brother for cutting so large a slice, their store of barley being low, but all he could think about was what present to ask for. "There are two trees by the well that lies at the world's end," said the cuckoo. "One of them is called the golden tree, for its leaves are all of beaten gold. Every winter they fall into the well, and I know not what becomes of them. As for the other, it is always green like a laurel. Some call it the wise, and some the merry, tree. Its leaves never fall, but those who get one of them keep a happy heart in spite of all misfortunes, and can make themselves as merry in a hut as in a palace."

"Good master cuckoo, bring me a leaf off that tree!" cried Spare.

"Now, brother, don't be a fool!" said Scrub; "think of the leaves of beaten gold! Dear master cuckoo, bring me one of them!"

Before another word could be spoken the cuckoo had flown out the open door, and was shouting its spring cry over moor and meadow.

The brothers were poorer than ever that year. Nobody would send them a single shoe to mend, and Scrub and Spare would have left the village but for their barley field and their cabbage garden. They sowed their barley, planted their cabbage, and now that their trade was gone, worked in the rich villagers' fields to make a scanty living.

So the seasons came and passed; spring, summer, harvest, and winter followed each other as they have done from the beginning. By the end of the latter Scrub and Spare had grown so poor and ragged that their old neighbors forgot to invite them to wedding feasts or merrymakings, and the brothers thought the cuckoo had forgotten them, too. But at daybreak on the first of April they heard a hard beak knocking at their door, and a voice crying: "Cuckoo! Cuckoo! Let me in with my presents!"

Spare ran to open the door, and in came the cuckoo, carrying on one side of its bill a golden leaf larger than that of any tree in the North Country; and in the other side of its bill, one like that of the common laurel, only it was a fresher green. "Here," it said, giving the gold to Scrub and the green to Spare, "it is a long carriage from the world's end. Give me a slice of barley bread, for I must tell the North Country that the spring has come."

Scrub did not grudge the thickness of that slice, though it was cut from their last loaf. So much gold had never been in the cobbler's hands before, and he could not help exulting over his brother. "See the wisdom of my choice," he said, holding up the large leaf of gold. "As for yours, as good might be plucked from any hedge. I wonder a sensible bird would carry the like so far."

"Good master cobbler," cried the cuckoo, "your conclusions are more hasty than courteous. If your brother is disappointed this time, I go on the same journey every year, and for your hospitality will think it no trouble to bring each of you whichever leaf you desire."

"Darling cuckoo," cried Scrub, "bring me a golden one." And Spare, looking up from the green leaf on which he gazed as though it were a crown jewel, said, "Be sure to bring me one from the merry tree."

And away flew the cuckoo.

"This is the feast of All Fools, and it ought to be your birthday," said Scrub. "Did ever a man fling away such an opportunity? Much good your merry leaves will do in the midst of rags and poverty!"

But Spare laughed at him, and answered with quaint old proverbs concerning the cares that come with gold, till Scrub, at length getting angry, vowed his brother was not fit to live with. And taking his lasts, his awls, and his golden leaf, he left the hut, and went to tell the villagers.

They were astonished at the folly of Spare and charmed with Scrub's good sense, particularly when he showed them the golden leaf and told them that the cuckoo would bring him one every spring.

The new cobbler immediately took him into partnership and the greatest people sent him their shoes to mend. Fairfeather, a beautiful village maiden, smiled graciously upon him; and in the course of that summer they were married. The whole village danced at their grand feast except Spare, who was not invited, because the bride could not bear his low-mindedness, and his brother thought him a disgrace to the family.

Scrub established himself with Fairfeather in a cottage close by that of the new cobbler, and quite as fine. There he mended shoes to everybody's satisfaction, had a scarlet coat, and a fat goose for dinner on holidays. Fairfeather, too, had a crimson gown and fine blue ribbons. But neither she nor Scrub was content, for to buy this grandeur the golden leaf had to be broken and parted with piece by piece, so the last morsel was gone before the cuckoo came with another.

Spare lived on in the old hut, and worked in the cabbage garden. (Scrub had got the barley field because he was the elder.) Every day his coat grew more ragged and the hut more weather-beaten, but people remarked that he never looked sad or sour. And the wonder was that, from the time anyone began to keep his company, he or she grew kinder, happier, and more content.

Every first of April the cuckoo came tapping at their doors with the golden leaf for Scrub and the green for Spare. Fairfeather would have entertained it nobly with wheaten bread and honey, for she had some notion of persuading it to bring two golden leaves instead of one. But the cuckoo flew away to eat barley bread with Spare, saying it was not fit company for fine people and liked the old hut where it slept so snugly from Christmas till spring.

Scrub spent the golden leaves and remained always discontented, and Spare kept the merry ones.

Many years passed in this manner, and then a certain great lord, who owned that village, came to the neighborhood. His castle stood on the moor. All the country as far as one could see from the highest turret of the castle belonged to its lord, but he had not been there for twenty years. He would not have come then only he was melancholy. The servants said nothing would please him, and the villagers put on their worst clothes lest he should raise their rents.

But one day in the harvest time his lordship chanced to meet Spare gathering water cresses at a meadow stream, and fell into talk with the cobbler. How it was nobody could tell, but from that hour the great lord cast away his melancholy. He forgot all his woes and went about with a noble train, hunting, fishing, and making merry in his hall.

This strange story spread through the North Country, and great company came to the cobbler's hut to talk with him—rich men who had lost their money, poor men who had lost their friends, beauties who had grown old, wits who had gone out of fashion. Whatever their troubles had been, all went home merry. The rich gave him presents and the poor gave him thanks.

Eventually his fame reached the capital city, and even the court. There were a great many discontented people there. And the king had lately fallen into ill humor because a neighboring princess, with seven islands for her dowry, would not marry his eldest son. So a royal messenger was sent to Spare with a velvet mantle, a diamond ring, and a command that he should report to court immediately.

"Tomorrow is the first of April," said Spare, "and I will go with you two hours after sunrise." The messenger lodged at the castle and at sunrise the cuckoo came with the merry leaf. "Court is a fine place," it said, when the cobbler told it he was going, "but I cannot come there. They would lay snares and catch me, so take care of the leaves I have brought you and give me a farewell slice of barley bread."

Spare was sorry to part with the cuckoo, little as he had of its company, but he gave it a slice which would have broken Scrub's heart in former times, it was so thick and large. And having sewed up the leaves in the lining of his leather doublet, he set out with the messenger on his way to court.

His coming caused great surprise there. Everybody wondered what the king could see in such a common-looking man. But scarcely had his majesty conversed with him half an hour, when the princess and her seven islands were forgotten and orders given that a feast for all comers should be spread in the banquet hall.

The lords forgot their spites and the ladies their envies, the princes and ministers made friends among themselves, and the judges showed no favor. As for Spare, he had a chamber assigned him in the palace, and a seat at the king's table. One sent him rich robes and another costly jewels, but in the midst of all his grandeur he still wore the leathern doublet. He continued to live at the king's court, happy and honored, and making all others merry and content.

December 18

Read Christmas Cards and Pray
for Those Who Sent Them

IN THE HUSTLE and bustle of a hectic holiday season, it's often easy to forget the needs of those around you. In the true spirit of celebrating the nature of Christ and His birth, try this important activity.

Gather all the Christmas cards you've received over the past weeks from beloved family and friends. Then set aside a special time as a family to pray specifically for each of the people represented, calling out their particular needs before the Father. In doing so, you will be honoring Christ and truly benefitting those for whom you are praying.

Father God,

We bring [family's name] before You, in Jesus' name, thanking You for meeting all of their needs according to Your riches in glory by Christ Jesus. (PHILIPPIANS 4:19.) *We pray that Your will is done in their lives and that You cause all things to work together for their good.* (ROMANS 8:28.)

Thank You that You have a good plan for their lives, a plan that will give them a hope and a future. (JEREMIAH 29:11.) *Lord, help them and give them peace in any decisions they may need to make. Thank You that they are Your sheep and they hear Your voice and they won't follow the voice of a stranger.* (JOHN 10:4-5,27.)

May they be filled with Your peace which passes understanding and watches over their hearts and minds. (PHILIPPIANS 4:7.) *And most of all, Lord, may they grow closer to You this holiday season and understand more than ever Your great love for them.*

Keep them safe from harm and close to one another and You.

In Jesus' name,

Amen ⁂

The Mistletoe Who Hated Kissing

Author Unknown

ONCE UPON A time, long, long ago, a king ruled a quaint kingdom in a green and fertile land. Now the king's family had a long tradition of royal gardening, which was their peaceful side, and of royal war-making, which was their definitely unpeaceful side.

The rose bushes in the queen's garden were very proud, descended from some of the earliest roses hundreds of years before brought from China and India, and the herb plants exhibited great dignity, as they could trace their roots back to cuttings first brought from Persia by Alexander the Great.

The King's personal grove of Christmas trees could remember back when they were merely pinecones, hearing the tales of the eldest trees of the journey from the Black Forest. Even the dandelions were elegant, and put on airs when their seeds blew away in the wind. But no one was more pompous than the garden of mistletoe which the Queen raised for Christmas, because she was inordinately fond of kissing the king.

Now, you may know about mistletoe at Christmas and kissing, but in case you don't, here is a quick review. It is a very old Christmas tradition to hang a spring of mistletoe over a doorway, or from a light in the center of the room. Anyone who stands under the mistletoe can be—or possibly, must be—kissed. Some people may spend the better part of Christmas just lurking in doorways, hoping that the right person will show up, ready to be kissed. It's one of those traditions that makes a great deal of sense from around the age of sixteen or so on up, but tends to be puzzling, if not downright gross, if you're much younger.

Now the Queen's mistletoe plants were the aristocrats of the garden, and their royal destiny to be cut for Christmas was considered the highest honor. But one year, the youngest mistletoe plant, whose education had been neglected, decided that he wouldn't be cut. "I can't stand mushy stuff," he said, "not hugging and certainly not kissing." So he grew around the oak tree where he was planted, higher and higher, trying to hide. When the official royal mistletoe cutters went into the garden, just before Christmas, he almost escaped. But they needed a great deal of mistletoe, for the castle had so many doorways, and just before they returned to the castle, he felt the quick cut of the shears, and whether he liked it or not, he was off to the royal chambers to be hung.

"No kissing!" he shouted into the gardeners' faces, but they completely ignored him, and as destiny and the whim of the Christmas decorating staff would have it, he ended up hung directly over the king's throne. The king wasn't celebrating Christmas at all, for he was arguing with a visiting prince, from a neighboring kingdom. *Great!* thought the young mistletoe, *fighting's much more fun than kissing.*

The two leaders argued about treaties and borders and who had rights to the river and the deer in the forest and anything else they could think of. All the while, the young mistletoe listened excitedly, wondering if they'd actually draw swords and fight a great duel.

Meanwhile, the queen was most put out, because this was a time of year when she had planned on kissing the king a great deal. But in spite of her hanging mistletoe everywhere—even right over his head in the throne room—he was far too busy arguing with that nice young prince from next door to pay her the least attention. So she assembled her staff of ten royal Christmas decorators, and the eleven royal ornament carriers, as well as the twelve official bearers of eggnog and the fifteen designated lords of cookie trays, and finally, the royal bearer for the queen's footstool. (She stood upon the footstool in order to be tall enough to kiss the king, for she was as short and round as the king was tall and skinny.). And the entire troop advanced into the king's throne room.

The ten royal Christmas decorators surrounded the king, as the eleven royal ornament carriers grouped themselves around the neighboring prince, while in between the two, the twelve official bearers of eggnog and the fifteen cookie tray lords all prepared refreshments for the assembled court. The youngest mistletoe was deeply disappointed, but the worst, he saw, was yet to come.

The Queen's stool bearer placed her stool next to the king, who was desperately trying to see where the prince was, behind and between all the servants, so that he could insult him one last time. Undaunted, the queen climbed up on her stool, planted a firm kiss on the King's lips, and proclaimed that all wars would be delayed at least a fortnight, for the holidays. The King and the mistletoe sighed deeply in unison, for it had looked to be a grand duel—although the neighboring Prince was secretly quite relieved.

Despite his disappointment at having to delay his great duel, the King kissed the Queen back and declared peace for a little while. At his declaration of peace, the young mistletoe was so upset that he flung himself off the golden hook above the king's throne, landed on the king's crown, and perched there, grumbling, for the rest of the Christmas season.

Which didn't bother the Queen—or reportedly the king, either—one bit.

December 19

Sing Christmas Hymns as a Family

ALTHOUGH MUCH OF Advent tradition is centered on the use of symbols, you can set aside time to sing special Christmas hymns along with your family as a beautiful verbal expression of the spirit of the season.

Keeping in mind Advent's focus on hope, joy, and expectation choose hymns that beautifully articulate these themes. *O Come, O Come, Emmanuel* is one favorite Advent hymn. *Joy to the World* is another. Have fun singing these meaningful hymns alone or with your family.

Heavenly Father,

We come before Your throne today in a spirit of worship. As we sing Christmas hymns together as a family, may we be reminded of the many wonderful miracles of Christmas. We glorify You, Lord, for Your everlasting love toward us and Your amazing plan to redeem us.

Lord, we pray in the words of Martin Luther,
All praise to Thee, eternal God,
Who, clothed in garb of flesh and blood,
Dost take a manger for Thy throne,
While worlds on worlds are Thine alone.
Hallelujah!

Thou comest in the darksome night
To make us children of the light,
To make us in the realms divine,
Like Thine own angels, round Thee shine.
Hallelujah!

All this for us Thy love hath done;
By this to Thee our love is won;
For this our joyful songs we raise
And shout our thanks in ceaseless praise.
Hallelujah!

Father God, You are so good to us. We praise Your holy name.

In Jesus' awesome name,

Amen ✳

The Story of "Silent Night"

Author Unknown

O N CHRISTMAS EVE, 1818, in the little Alpine village of Oberndorf in northern Austria, it was snowing hard. The people of the little town had long before gone to bed and all was quiet and still. But there was one light still burning. It shone from the study window of the young priest, Joseph Mohr.

Joseph had not been able to go to sleep that night and he had been pacing up and down his study floor, pausing now and then to look out the window at the silent, snow-covered scene before him. He was deeply worried. Christmas, a day of music and rejoicing, was almost there and as yet he had seen no way to overcome the disappointment he knew was in store for his congregation.

The church organ was in desperate need of repair and there was no repairman in the town of Oberndorf, and the heavy snows had made it impossible to get one from anywhere else.

He was thinking of this and at the same time was remembering a conversation he had had the preceding summer with his friend, Franz Gruber, a schoolteacher in the town of Arnsdorf not far away. Gruber was also an accomplished musician and played the organ in the village church.

One day, as was their custom, they had been sitting in the pastor's garden singing together to the accompaniment of Gruber's guitar. Suddenly Gruber had stopped in the middle of a hymn and turned to his friend. "Father," he had said, "do you realize that of all these Christmas songs we've been singing none expresses the real Christmas spirit?"

"You are right, my friend," the priest answered. "Perhaps one day someone will write a song that will tell simply the meaning of the Holy Night."

"Why should not that someone be you?" asked the schoolmaster. Joseph Mohr had laughed. "And will you write the music if I do?"

"Of course," Gruber replied. "And I'm quite serious about this. I'm sure you can do it."

In the weeks that followed this conversation, Joseph Mohr had tried to write that song. But somehow, try as he would, the words simply didn't come. Now, on Christmas Eve, he felt a little sad as he thought of the service the next evening with no organ and no new song to sing to his people as he had planned.

As he stood at his window now, lost in thought, he suddenly realized that someone was struggling through the deep snow toward his house. He rushed to the door and went out to help his exhausted visitor into the warmth of his fire. It was a woman, too breathless to speak for some moments, but at last she was able to tell her story.

She had come over the mountain from the cabin of a friend of hers who that night had given birth to her first child, a son. "And Father," the woman concluded, "her husband, who is a young woodcutter, is very anxious that you come and bless the new mother and the babe this very night."

"Of course I'll go." the priest answered.

"But the snow is getting very deep," the woman protested. "I came as I promised him I would, but I'm sure he'll understand if you wait until morning. 'Twas not snowing hard like this when I left their house."

"I don't mind the snow. And the walk will be good for me," Joseph answered. "I'm feeling too wakeful to go to bed anyway. You stay here and rest before you go home."

Joseph bundled himself up in his warmest clothes and grabbed a stout cane to help him, and then he started out in the cold winter night. It was several miles to the woodcutter's cabin and the heavy snow made it difficult to walk, but when he arrived and opened the door his breath caught at the scene before him.

There was the new mother in her bed smiling happily at her husband, who was kneeling in adoration before a crude wooden crib in which lay his newborn son. It seemed to Joseph Mohr that he was looking at a scene that had taken place in Bethlehem of Judea many ages before.

The young woodcutter felt the sudden draft of cold air and rose quickly to his feet. "Welcome, Father," he cried. "I didn't expect you to come when I realized how hard it was snowing, but I'm grateful you're here."

Proudly he led the priest over to the cradle where the child lay and Father Mohr admired the baby and then gave him and the mother his blessing.

Although the woodcutter wanted the priest to partake of some refreshment before he left, Father Mohr replied that he must be on his way. Bidding good-bye to the happy parents, he set out for home—but this time the way didn't seem quite so hard. The snow was no longer falling, but the branches of the pine trees bent low under their heavy white mantle. The stillness in the forest was awe-inspiring. As he plowed through the drifts the pastor kept thinking of the little family he had just left. Truly this had been a holy night.

At home, he could hardly wait to take off his coat and warm his stiff fingers. Then he sat down at his desk and began to write. It was early morning before he finished and fell exhausted upon his bed for a little rest.

But he didn't stay there long. Soon he arose, ate his breakfast, and hurried out again. This time he went in the direction of Arnsdorf where his friend Franz Gruber lived. When Gruber opened his door Joseph

Mohr handed him the manuscript containing the words he had written in the early morning hours.

Silent Night

Silent night, Holy night,
All is calm, all is bright
'Round yon virgin mother and child!
Holy infant so tender and mild,
Sleep in heavenly peace,
Sleep in heavenly peace.

Silent night, Holy night
Shepherds quake at the sight
Glories stream from heaven afar,
Heavenly hosts sing "Alleluia"
Christ the Savior is born.
Christ the Savior is born.

Silent night, Holy night
Son of God, love's pure light
Radiant beams from Thy holy face
With the dawn of redeeming grace.
Jesus, Lord at thy birth.
Jesus, Lord at thy birth.

December 20

Special Scripture Reading

BROADEN YOUR UNDERSTANDING and amazement at the miraculous birth of Christ during this Advent by reading aloud familiar passages of scripture such as the Old Testament prophecies of Christ's birth. Psalms and Isaiah are both great places to begin your journey.

Then, read the first chapter of the Gospel of John, where Jesus is described as coming as a light to the world. Many of the beloved traditions of Advent use candles and candlelight as central symbols of Jesus and His birth. This familiar chapter will instill a deeper understanding and significance into each of those traditions.

Father God,

We are in awe of Your great love today. To know that You planned from before the foundations of the earth to redeem us and make us Your children is the greatest blessing we could receive this Christmas season. We rejoice in Your loving-kindness and compassion. We praise You for Your amazing grace and tender mercies.

There is no God like You. No Father could possibly love us more, for You are love. Thank You that we have been adopted, chosen by You to be Your children, and no one can ever pluck us out of Your hand. (JOHN 10:29.)

Lord, as we prepare our hearts to receive Your Christmas gifts, we ask that You forgive all our sins and trespasses. We thank You that You are faithful and just to forgive us all of our sins and to cleanse us from all our trespasses. (1 JOHN 1:9.) *Thank You that we can be made clean and pure and holy in Your sight. We want to walk in the path of righteousness because we want to please You, our loving, gracious, merciful, compassionate, slow-to-anger Father God.*

We bless Your name, O God.

In Jesus' name,

Amen ❄

Old Testament Prophecies of Jesus Birth

A Virgin Will Conceive

"The Lord himself will choose the sign. Look! The virgin will conceive a child! She will give birth to a son and will call him Immanuel— 'God is with us.'"

ISAIAH 7:14 NLT

To Us a Child Is Born

HE PEOPLE WALKING in darkness have seen a great light; on those living in the land of the shadow of death a light has dawned.

"You have enlarged the nation and increased their joy; they rejoice before you as people rejoice at the harvest, as men rejoice when dividing the plunder.

"For as in the day of Midian's defeat, you have shattered the yoke that burdens them, the bar across their shoulders, the rod of their oppressor.

"Every warrior's book used in battle and every garment rolled in blood will be destined for burning, will be fuel for the fire.

"For to us a child is born, to us a son is given, and the government will be on his shoulders. And he will be called Wonderful Counselor, Mighty God, Everlasting Father, Prince of Peace.

"Of the increase of his government and peace there will be no end. He will reign on David's throne and over his kingdom, establishing and upholding it with justice and righteousness from that time on and forever.

"The zeal of the LORD Almighty will accomplish this."

ISAIAH 9:2-7

The Branch from Jesse

"Like a branch that sprouts from a stump, someone from David's family will someday be king. The Spirit of the LORD will be with him to give him understanding, wisdom, and insight. He will be powerful, and he will know and honor the LORD.

"His greatest joy will be to obey the LORD. This king won't judge by appearances or listen to rumors. The poor and the needy will be treated with fairness and with justice. His word will be law everywhere in the land, and criminals will be put to death. Honesty and fairness will be his royal robes.

'Leopards will lie down with young goats, and wolves will rest with lambs. Calves and lions will eat together and be cared for by little children. Cows and bears will share the same pasture; their young will rest side by side. Lions and oxen will both eat straw. Little children will play near snake holes. They will stick their hands into dens of poisonous snakes and never be hurt.

> "Nothing harmful will take place on the LORD's holy mountain. Just as water fills the sea, the land will be filled with people who know and honor the LORD."

ISAIAH 11:1-9 CEV

His Birth in Bethlehem

> "But you, Bethlehem Ephrathah, though you are small among the clans of Judah, out of you will come for me one who will be ruler over Israel, whose origins are from of old, from ancient times."

MICAH 5:2

The Decree of the Lord

> "I will proclaim the decree of the Lord: He said to me, 'You are my Son; today I have become your Father. Ask of me, and I will make the nations your inheritance, the ends of the earth your possession.'"

PSALM 2:7-8

The Messiah Will Rule

"The Lord said to my Lord, 'Sit in honor at my right hand until I humble your enemies, making them a footstool under your feet.'

"The Lord will extend your powerful dominion from Jerusalem; you will rule over your enemies.

"In that day of battle, your people will serve you willingly. Arrayed in holy garments, your vigor will be renewed each day like the morning dew.

"The Lord has taken an oath and will not break his vow: 'You are a priest forever in the line of Melchizedek.'

"The Lord stands at your right hand to protect you. He will strike down many kings in the day of his anger.

"He will punish the nations and fill them with their dead; he will shatter heads over the whole earth. But he himself will be refreshed from brooks along the way.

"He will be victorious."

PSALM 110 NLT

Jesus Is the Light of the World

The Word Became Flesh

"In the beginning was the Word, and the Word was with God, and the Word was God. He was with God in the beginning.

"Through him all things were made; without him nothing was made that has been made. In him was life, and that life was the light of men. The light shines in the darkness, but the darkness has not understood it.

"There came a man who was sent from God; his name was John. He came as a witness to testify concerning that light, so that through him all men might believe. He himself was not the light; he came only as a witness to the light. The true light that gives light to every man was coming into the world.

"He was in the world, and though the world was made through him, the world did not recognize him. He came to that which was his own, but his own did not receive him. Yet to all who received him, to those who believed in his name, he gave the right to become children of God—children born not of natural descent, nor of human decision or a husband's will, but born of God.

"The Word became flesh and made his dwelling among us. We have seen his glory, the glory of the One and Only, who came from the Father, full of grace and truth.

"John testifies concerning him. He cries out, saying, "This was he of whom I said, 'He who comes after me has surpassed me because he was before me'." From the fullness of his grace we have all received one blessing after another. For the law was given through Moses; grace and truth came through Jesus Christ. No one has ever seen God, but God the One and Only, who is at the Father's side, has made him known."

JOHN 1:1-18

December 21

Bake Special Advent Breads

FILL YOUR HOME with the pungent aroma of baking breads as you spend the final days in preparation for the celebration of Christ's birth. Try your hand at Brioche, Christstollen, or Melachrino—three traditional advent breads with special significance. Recipes for each can easily be found on the internet or in holiday cookbooks.

Brioche, or French Christmas bread, is very light, rich bread that is delightful served warm right out of the oven. Christstollen, a bread of German origin, is unique because its criss-cross shape reminds us of baby Jesus in swaddling clothes. Melachrino is a delicious Greek sweet bread that hides a special surprise. It is customary to serve this bread with a silver coin hidden deep in its crust.

Enjoy the experience of trying these new recipes with your family. They are sure to become favorites for years to come!

Father God,

We hunger and thirst after You today. You are the bread of life and the well of salvation. We thank You for providing living bread, that we might not hunger, and living water that we might not thirst. Your Word is life to our flesh and healing to all our bones. The words that You speak to us are spirit and they are life. (JOHN 6:63.)

Lord, we also thank You for our daily bread. Thank You for Your wonderful provision for our family. We pray that we might share our provision of bread with others in need. Lead us to someone today with whom we can share, not only natural bread, but also the true Bread of Life.

We remember the sacrament of communion and the bread that represents the body of Jesus, broken for us. He was wounded for our transgressions and bruised for our iniquities, the chastisement of our peace was upon him, and by his stripes we are healed. (ISAIAH 53:5.) *We praise You, Father God, that we have been made whole in spirit, soul, and body through the gift of Your Son.*

Thank You for Your precious gift.

In Jesus' name,

Amen ⁂

The Stranger Child

By Count Franz Pocci

THERE ONCE LIVED a laborer who earned his daily bread by cutting wood. His wife and two children, a boy and girl, helped him with his work. The boy's name was Valentine, and the girl's, Marie. They were obedient and pious and the joy and comfort of their poor parents.

One winter evening, this good family gathered about the table to eat their small loaf of bread, while the father read aloud from the Bible. Just as they sat down there came a knock on the window, and a sweet voice called, "O let me in! I am a little child, and I have nothing to eat, and no place to sleep in. I am so cold and hungry! Please, good people, let me in!"

Valentine and Marie sprang from the table and ran to open the door, saying, "Come in, poor child, we have but very little ourselves, not much more than you have, but what we have we will share with you."

The stranger Child entered, and going to the fire began to warm his cold hands. The children gave him a portion of their bread, and said, "You must be very tired; come, lie down in our bed, and we will sleep on the bench here before the fire."

Then answered the stranger Child: "May God in Heaven reward you for your kindness."

They led the little guest to their small room, laid him in their bed, and covered him closely, thinking to themselves, *Oh! how much we have to be thankful for! We have our nice warm room and comfortable bed, while this Child has nothing but the sky for a roof, and the earth for a couch.*

When the parents went to their bed, Valentine and Marie lay down on the bench before the fire, and said one to the other, "The stranger Child is happy now, because he is so warm! Good-night!"

Then they fell asleep.

They had not slept many hours, when little Marie awoke, and touching her brother lightly, whispered, "Valentine, Valentine, wake up! wake up! Listen to the beautiful music at the window."

Valentine rubbed his eyes and listened. He heard the most wonderful singing and the sweet notes of many harps.

Blessed Child,
Thee we greet,
With sound of harp
And singing sweet.

Sleep in peace,
Child so bright,
We have watched Thee
All the night

Blest the home
That holdeth Thee,
Peace, and love,
Its guardians be."

The children listened to the beautiful singing, and it seemed to fill them with unspeakable happiness. Then they crept quietly to the window and looked out.

They saw a rosy light in the east, and, before the house in the snow, stood a number of little children holding golden harps and lutes in their hands, and dressed in sparkling, silver robes.

Full of wonder at this sight, Valentine and Marie continued to gaze out at the window, when they heard a sound behind them. When they turned, they saw the stranger Child standing near. He was clad in a golden garment and wore a glistening, golden crown upon His soft hair. Sweetly He spoke to the children,

"I am the Christ Child, who wanders about the world seeking to bring joy and good things to loving children. Because you have lodged Me this night I will leave with you My blessing."

As the Christ Child spoke He stepped from the door, and breaking off a bough from a fir tree that grew near, planted it in the ground, saying, "This bough shall grow into a tree, and every year it shall bear Christmas fruit for you."

Having said this He vanished from their sight, together with the silver-clad, singing children—the angels.

As Valentine and Marie looked on in wonder, the fir bough grew, and grew, and grew, into a stately Christmas tree laden with golden apples, silver nuts, and lovely toys. And after that, every year at Christmastime, the tree bore the same wonderful fruit.

And you, dear boys and girls, when you gather around your richly decorated trees, think of the two poor children who shared their bread with a stranger child, and be thankful.

December 22

Lighting the Fourth Candle
of the Advent Wreath

THE FOURTH CANDLE of the Advent wreath symbolizes love and is a reminder that it was through God's great love for us that Jesus came to earth. Gather your family for a special time of reflecting on this love as you light the candle together.

Read John 3 and think of ways that God's love has been expressed to you. Then, pray together that you will each be filled with the love of God and willing to follow Jesus' example in sharing it with all those around you.

Father God,

We are grateful for Your overwhelming love. You loved us so much that You sent Your only begotten Son to die for us, to pay the price that we were not capable of paying. You gave that which was precious and dear to You, in order to have us, who are also precious and dear to You. There is nothing in this world or out of this world, that can compare with Your love.

May we truly manifest Your love to those around us this season. Help us to grow in our understanding of Your love for us, and in our practice of sharing Your love with others. Help us to see others the way You do, with love. Remind us daily of all the things love is, and does. As You are patient with us, may be we patient with others. As you are kind to us, may we be kind to others. May we learn to truly love.

Lord, help us to treat people with love and respect, not judgment or anger. Lord, we set our hearts on You and as we do, we purpose to allow Your love to flow through us to everyone in need of Your gentle, loving touch.

In Jesus' name,

Amen ⁕

The Love of God

John 3 CEV

THERE WAS A man named Nicodemus who was a Pharisee and a Jewish leader. One night he went to Jesus and said, "Sir, we know that God has sent you to teach us. You could not work these miracles, unless God were with you."

Jesus replied, "I tell you for certain that you must be born from above before you can see God's kingdom!"

Nicodemus asked, "How can a grown man ever be born a second time?"

Jesus answered: I tell you for certain that before you can get into God's kingdom, you must be born not only by water, but by the Spirit. Humans give life to their children. Yet only God's Spirit can change you into a child of God. Don't be surprised when I say that you must be born from above. Only God's Spirit gives new life. The Spirit is like the wind that blows wherever it wants to. You can hear the wind, but you don't know where it comes from or where it is going.

"How can this be?" Nicodemus asked.

Jesus replied: How can you be a teacher of Israel and not know these things? I tell you for certain that we know what we are talking about because we have seen it ourselves. But none of you will accept what we say.

If you don't believe when I talk to you about things on earth, how can you possibly believe if I talk to you about things in heaven? No one has gone up to heaven except the Son of Man, who came down from there. And the Son of Man must be lifted up, just as that metal snake was lifted up by Moses in the desert. Then everyone who has faith in the Son of Man will have eternal life.

God loved the people of this world so much that he gave his only Son, so that everyone who has faith in him will have eternal life and never really die.

God did not send his Son into the world to condemn its people. He sent him to save them!

No one who has faith in God's Son will be condemned. But everyone who doesn't have faith in him has already been condemned for not having faith in God's only Son.

The light has come into the world, and people who do evil things are judged guilty because they love the dark more than the light. People who do evil hate the light and won't come to the light, because it clearly shows what they have done.

But everyone who lives by the truth will come to the light, because they want others to know that God is really the one doing what they do.

Later, Jesus and his disciples went to Judea, where he stayed with them for a while and was baptizing people. John had not yet been put in jail. He was at Aenon near Salim, where there was a lot of water, and people were coming there for John to baptize them.

John's followers got into an argument with a Jewish man about a ceremony of washing. They went to John and said, "Rabbi, you spoke about a man when you were with him east of the Jordan. He is now baptizing people, and everyone is going to him."

John replied: No one can do anything unless God in heaven allows it. You surely remember how I told you that I am not the Messiah. I am only the one sent ahead of him. At a wedding the groom is the one who gets married. The best man is glad just to be there and to hear the groom's voice. That's why I am so glad.

Jesus must become more important, while I become less important. God's Son comes from heaven and is above all others. Everyone who comes from the earth belongs to the earth and speaks about earthly things. The one who comes from heaven is above all others. He speaks about what he has seen and heard, and yet no one believes him. But everyone who does believe him has shown that God is truthful.

The Son was sent to speak God's message, and he has been given the full power of God's Spirit. The Father loves the Son and has given him everything. Everyone who has faith in the Son has eternal life. But no one who rejects him will ever share in that life, and God will be angry with them forever.

"God's love can always be trusted, and his faithfulness lasts as long as the heavens."

PSALM 89:2 CEV

"I am convinced that neither death nor life, neither angels nor demons, neither the present nor the future, nor any powers, neither height nor depth, nor anything else in all creation, will be able to separate us from the love of God that is in Christ Jesus our Lord."

ROMANS 8:38-39

December 23

Create Your Own Family Tradition Commemorating the Advent Season

THE MOST MEANINGFUL holiday traditions are usually those that have been passed down from generation to generation. Tap into your family's rich and unique heritage by creating your own priceless commemoration of the Advent season.

Reflect upon the true spirit of the Advent season as you gather your family and let your collective creative juices flow! Your new tradition can be as simple as a family craft project or a shared dish or as elaborate as a family play. Enjoy this time spent together as you institute a special tradition sure to be treasured for years to come.

Heavenly Father,

We thank You for the gift of tradition, those things we can count on year after year to remind us of the true reason we celebrate Christmas. We ask You to give us wisdom in beginning a new family tradition that would speak to our family of Your amazing gift for generations to come.

Lord, we know that it is important to You for us to pass Your words, Your commands, Your ways to our children. May this Christmas season, and every one to come, be a special, meaningful time of sharing our faith in a memorable way with our family.

Lord, we truly want to serve You with our whole hearts this Christmas. Help us to remain in that spirit of love. Whenever the business of the season weighs upon us, remind us what it's all about. As we stop and magnify You, renew our focus. You alone are holy and worthy of all our praise and adoration.

In Jesus' name,

Amen ❋

Mike's Christmas Legacy

Author Unknown

IT'S JUST A small, white envelope stuck among the branches of our Christmas tree. No name, no identification, no inscription. It has peeked through the branches of our tree for the past ten years or so.

It all began because my husband Mike hated Christmas—oh, not the true meaning of Christmas, but the commercial aspects of it—overspending, the frantic running around at the last minute to get a tie for Uncle Harry and the dusting powder for Grandma, the gifts given in desperation because you couldn't think of anything else.

Knowing he felt this way, I decided one year to bypass the usual shirts, sweaters, ties, and so forth. I searched for something special just for Mike. The inspiration came in an unusual way.

Our son Kevin, who was twelve that year, was wrestling at the junior level at the school he attended. Shortly before Christmas, there was a non-league match against a team sponsored by an inner-city church.

These youngsters, dressed in sneakers so ragged that shoestrings seemed to be the only thing holding them together, presented a sharp contrast to our boys in their spiffy blue and gold uniforms and sparkling new wrestling shoes. As the match began, I was alarmed to see that the other team was wrestling without headgear, a kind of light helmet designed to protect a wrestler's ears. It was a luxury the ragtag team obviously could not afford. Well, we ended up walloping them.

We took every weight class. But as each of their boys got up from the mat, he swaggered around in his tatters with false bravado, a kind of street pride that couldn't acknowledge defeat. Mike, seated beside me, shook his head sadly, "I wish just one of them could have won," he said. "They have a lot of potential, but losing like this could take the heart right out of them."

Mike loved kids—all kids—and he knew them, having coached Little League football, baseball, and lacrosse. That's when the idea for his present came. That afternoon, I went to a local sporting goods store and bought an assortment of wrestling headgear and shoes and sent them anonymously to the inner-city church.

On Christmas Eve, I placed the envelope on the tree, the note inside telling Mike what I had done and that this was his gift from me. His smile was the brightest thing about Christmas that year and in succeeding years. For each Christmas, I followed the tradition—one year sending a group of mentally handicapped youngsters to a hockey game, another year a check to a pair of elderly brothers whose home had burned to the ground the week before Christmas, and on and on.

The envelope became the highlight of our Christmas. It was always the last thing opened on Christmas morning and our children, ignoring their new toys, would stand with wide-eyed anticipation as their dad lifted the envelope from the tree to reveal its contents. As the children grew, the toys gave way to more practical presents, but the envelope never lost its allure. The story doesn't end there.

You see, we lost Mike last year due to dreaded cancer.

When Christmas rolled around, I was still so wrapped in grief that I barely got the tree up. But Christmas Eve found me placing an envelope on the tree, and in the morning, it was joined by three more.

Each of our children, unbeknownst to the others, had placed an envelope on the tree for their dad. The tradition has grown and someday will expand even further with our grandchildren standing around the tree with wide-eyed anticipation watching as their fathers take down the envelope. Mike's spirit, like the Christmas spirit, will always be with us.

May we all remember each other, and their interpretation of the true Reason for the season, and the true spirit this year and always.

December 24

Decorate the Christ Candle for the Center of the Advent Wreath

WITH THE CELEBRATION of Christ's birth only one day away, take time to center your focus a final time on the joyful anticipation of His coming by decorating the Christ candle to be used in the center of your Advent wreath.

The Christ candle is usually a larger white candle and will be positioned in the center of the Advent wreath. Be creative and engage your entire family in the task, as you use common crafting supplies like paint, ribbon, and beads to adorn your candle. The result will be a beautiful addition to your special celebration on Christmas Day.

Heavenly Father,

There is something magical about Christmas Eve—the anticipation and excitement of giving and receiving gifts. All the world feels at peace, somehow. Tonight, may we see the wonder of Your creation. The amazing world You've created for us to live in, and remember the miraculous signs of Jesus' birth that night so long ago.

As we look at the stars, may we remember the one star that led the shepherds and later the wise men to worship Jesus. We say with David, "When I consider your heavens, the works of your fingers, the moon and the stars, which you have set in place, what is man that you are mindful of him, the son of man that you care for him?" (PSALM 8:3-4.) Yet we know that You do care for us, You are mindful of us. We are wrapped in Your loving care.

As we look at the snow, (or dream of it), may we be reminded that though our sins be as scarlet, You have made them whiter than snow. (ISAIAH 1:18.) As we look at the evergreen Christmas tree, may we be reminded of the everlasting life You have given us. May the red berries of the holly, and the red of Christmas bows and decorations remind us of Jesus' blood, shed for us—the ultimate purpose of His coming into this world as a baby in a manger. Lord, may we always remember.

In Jesus' name,

Amen ✳

The Christmas Truce of 1914

Author Unknown

ON CHRISTMAS EVE in the winter of 1914, during a war that took eight-and-a-half million souls, a most unusual event took place on the battlefields of Flanders. The British had been in a fierce battle with the Germans, and both sides were dug in and resolute, holed-up in deep, mud-filled trenches that seemed to stretch all the way to Hell. All about them it was cold and dark, the memories of fallen comrades and the fears of battles to come weighing heavy on their minds.

No one now is quite sure how it started. Perhaps a single German soldier looked up and saw a star. Perhaps he thought of Baby Jesus and remembered the meaning of this night and reminded his troops. But we do know that something that holy night inspired the German troops to put small Christmas trees, lit with candles, outside of their trenches. Then, they began to sing. "Stille Nacht! Heil'ge Nacht! Alles schläft, einsam wacht…."

The British heard the singing and were confused. They looked across the way, over the icy "no man's land" that separated them from their enemy, and saw the golden fire of candles lighting up trees like winter fireflies. What a strange and lovely sight it must've been to see such a thing in the middle of a moonlit, bloodied battlefield! Through the wintry darkness shone a symbol of Christ!

One of the British must've been the first to begin to sing in response. One man must've heard the Germans' singing and so felt the peace of Christ that he was drawn to join in. It had to start somewhere. But, in any case, soon enough, the Germans across the way could clearly hear their enemy singing the words of a different carol, an English one: "The first Noel, the angels did say…."

The Germans applauded! Yes, they applauded, and then they began to sing a third carol, "O Tannenbaum, O Tannenbaum…"—to which the British replied with "Adeste Fideles, Laeti triumphantes, Venite, venite in Bethlehem…." Ah, Latin! This the Germans knew, too! They could sing together! And they did. The German voices and British voices harmonizing and imploring all, "O Come, let us adore Him!"

Then the Germans put up signs in fractured English: "YOU NO SHOOT, WE NO SHOOT." Some British units improvised "MERRY CHRIST-MAS" banners and waited for a response. More plac-ards popped up on both sides. The Germans proposed a Christmas truce, and, all along the miles of trenches, the British troops accepted. In a few places, allied troops fired at the Germans as they climbed out of their trenches, but the Germans were persistent— Christmas would be celebrated even under the threat of impending death.

Soldiers left their trenches and met in the middle of that frosty "No Man's Land" to shake hands. The first order of business was to bury the dead who had been previously unreachable because of the conflict. Then they made gifts of the things sent from home— chocolate cake, plum puddings, cognac, coffee, butterscotches, tobacco, postcards. In a few places along the trenches, soldiers exchanged rifles for soccer balls and began to play games.

It didn't last forever. In fact, some of the generals didn't like it at all and commanded their troops to resume shooting at each other. After all, they were in a war. Soldiers eventually did resume shooting at each other—but only after a few days of wasting rounds of ammunition shooting at stars in the sky instead of at soldiers in the opposing army across the field.

For a few precious moments there was peace on earth, and all because men's hearts were filled with the spirit of Christmas. There's something about this holy season that changes people. It happened over two millennia ago in a little town called Bethlehem, and it's been happening, over and over again, ever since.

This season, God willing, it will happen again.

December 25

Lighting the Christ Candle in the Center of the Advent Wreath

THE CONCLUSION OF the Advent season should be a fulfilling culmination of the past weeks spent in anticipation of the celebration of Christ's birth. With a heart full of genuine gratitude at the priceless gift God gave in sending His only Son, gather your family to savor the lighting of the final candle of the Advent wreath—the Christ Candle.

The Christ candle is usually positioned in the center of the wreath and should be added to the wreath on Christmas Day. It serves as a poignant symbol of His virgin birth, resurrection, and future return. Ask each member of your family to share an observation about the nature of Christ as you conclude the Advent season with hearts full of thankfulness and joy for all He's done.

Father God,

We come before You today in the humble spirit of the shepherds—in awe of your gracious Gift.

May we begin this Christmas Day in its true spirit—a spirit of giving and receiving. For You gave us the Gift of Your only begotten Son, so that we could believe on Him and receive eternal life. (JOHN 3:16.)

But this wonderful Gift is for naught if we don't receive it. Jesus came to give. He endured the cross and its shame because of the joy set before Him—that we would receive His Gift. (HEBREWS 12:2.)

We come to You today thankful for that Gift. As we give and receive gifts and enjoy our family today, may we truly understand the significance of Your Gift and our place in Your family.

May we begin to understand the fullness of Jesus' love for us and grow to love Him more, listen to His voice, and obey His words. May we become firmly rooted in His love.

Just as Jesus knew His purpose—His reason for being put on this planet—I pray that each of us would know our purpose and begin to walk in it more and more.

Thank You for the opportunity to bless someone today. May we cross paths with someone less fortunate—in friends, family, or finances—and meet their need out of the abundance of our blessing.

In Jesus' wonderful name,

Amen

On the Morning of Christ's Nativity

By John Milton

THIS IS THE month, and this the happy morn
Wherein the Son of Heav'n's eternal King,
Of wedded Maid, and Virgin Mother born,
Our great redemption from above did bring;
For so the holy sages once did sing,
That He our deadly forfeit should release,
And with His Father work us a perpetual peace.

II

That glorious Form, that Light unsufferable,
And that far-beaming blaze of Majesty,
Wherewith He wont at Heav'n's high council table,
To sit in the midst of Trinal Unity,
He laid aside, and here with us to be,
Forsook the courts of everlasting day,
And chose with us a darksome house of mortal clay.

III

Say Heav'nly Muse, shall not thy sacred vein
Afford a present to the Infant God?
Hast thou no verse, no hymn, or solemn strain,
To welcome Him to this His new abode,
Now while the heav'n, by the Sun's team untrod,
Hath took no print of the approaching light,
And all the spangled host keep watch in squadrons
　　bright?

IV

See how from far upon the eastern road
The star-led [wise men] haste with odors sweet:
O run, prevent them with thy humble ode,
And lay it lowly at His blessed feet;
Have thou the honor first thy Lord to greet,
And join thy voice unto the angel quire,
From out His secret altar touched with hallowed
　　fire.

The Hymn
I

It was the winter wild,
While the Heav'n-born child,
All meanly wrapt in the rude manger lies;
Nature in awe to Him
Had doffed her gaudy trim,
With her great Master so to sympathize:
It was no season then for her
To wanton with the Sun, her lusty paramour.

II

Only with speeches fair
She woos the gentle air
To hide her guilty front with innocent snow,
And on her naked shame,
Pollute with sinful blame,
The saintly veil of maiden white to throw,
Confounded, that her Maker's eyes
Should look so near upon her foul deformities.

III

But He, her fears to cease,
Sent down the meek-eyed Peace:
She, crowned with olive green, came softly sliding
Down through the turning sphere,
His ready harbinger,
With turtle wing the amorous clouds dividing;
And waving wide her myrtle wand,
She strikes a universal peace through sea and land.

IV

No war or battle's sound
Was heard the world around;
The idle spear and shield were high uphung;
The hooked chariot stood
Unstained with hostile blood;
The trumpet spake not to the armed throng;
And kings sat still with awful eye,
As if they surely knew their sovereign Lord was by.

V

But peaceful was the night
Wherein the Prince of Light
His reign of peace upon the earth began:
The winds with wonder whist,
Smoothly the waters kist,
Whispering new joys to the mild Ocean,
Who now hath quite forgot to rave,
While birds of calm sit brooding on the charmed
    wave.

VI

The Stars with deep amaze
Stand fixed in steadfast gaze,
Bending one way their precious influence;
And will not take their flight,
For all the morning light,
Or Lucifer that often warned them thence,
But in their glimmering orbs did glow,
Until their Lord Himself bespake, and bid them go.

VII

And though the shady gloom
Had given day her room,
The Sun himself withheld his wonted speed,
And hid his head for shame,
As his inferior flame
The new-enlightened world no more should need:
He saw a greater Sun appear
Than his bright throne or burning axle-tree could
    bear.

VIII

When such music sweet
Their hearts and ears did greet,
As never was by mortal finger strook,
Divinely warbled voice
Answering the stringed noise,
As all their souls in blissful rapture took:
The air such pleasure loth to lose,
With thousand echoes still prolongs each heav'nly
    close…

XI

…At last surrounds their sight
A globe of circular light,
That with long beams the shame-faced Night arrayed;
The helmed Cherubim
And sworded Seraphim
Are seen in glittering ranks with wings displayed,
Harping in loud and solemn quire,
With unexpressive notes to Heav'n's newborn Heir.

XII

Such music (as 'tis said)
Before was never made,
But when of old the sons of morning sung,
While the Creator great
His constellations set,
And the well-balanced world on hinges hung,
And cast the dark foundations deep,
And bid the welt'ring waves their oozy channel
    keep.

XIII

Ring out ye crystal spheres!
Once bless our human ears
(If ye have power to touch our senses so)
And let your silver chime
Move in melodious time,
And let the bass of Heav'n's deep organ blow;
And with your ninefold harmony
Make up full consort to th' angelic symphony....

XXVII

...But see, the Virgin blest
Hath laid her Babe to rest:
Time is our tedious song should here have ending.
Heav'n's youngest-teemed star,
Hath fixed her polished ear,
Her sleeping Lord with handmaid lamp attending;
And all about the courtly stable,
Bright-harnessed Angels sit in order serviceable.

Additional copies of this book
are available from your local bookstore.

Visit our website at:
www.whitestonebooks.com

If you have enjoyed this book
we would love to hear from you.
Please write us at:
White Stone Books
Department E
1501 South Florida Avenue
Lakeland, Florida 33803

WHITE STONE BOOKS
LAKELAND, FLORIDA